D0553276

COVERING MY TRACKS

COVERING MY TRACKS

Recollections of the end of steam

Robert Adley

GUILD PUBLISHING LONDON

© Robert Adley 1988

This edition published 1988 by Guild Publishing by arrangement with Patrick Stephens Limited

The coloured maps in this book are reproduced from the Sixth Edition of *Railway Junction Diagrams* by John Airey of the Railway Clearing House, published in 1888 with its supplement dated 1892. Obviously, in the intervening century the railway system has fundamentally changed, but these old maps are colourful, informative and historically interesting — hence their inclusion in this book. The illustration on page 69 is reproduced from Parliamentary Papers in the House of Commons Library. All the colour photographs were taken by the author.

Printed in Italy by New Interlitho, Milan. Colour reproduction by Royle Print, London.

ACKNOWLEDGEMENTS

To Kay Dixon, for endless patience and ingenuity both in deciphering my illegible scrawl and interpreting my errant search for information; to Peter Semmens for correcting and for assisting in the elimination of some of the errors, omissions and inaccuracies in the manuscript; to those authors and historians whose scholarship where appropriate has been acknowledged in the text; to British Rail for their unfailing patience and help, and of course to their past and present employees for guidance and assistance; and to my family, whose members, both two and four legged, 'lose' one member of the family, at home occasionally 'twixt Parliamentary duties, to the lure of 'the book'.

Dedication

To Sam, Tom, George and Oscar

Title page *By 4 February 1964, when this photograph was taken, March shed had officially closed to steam, but the message had not reached the ears of 'WD' Austerity 2-8-0 No 90111, or LNER 'B1' 4-6-0 No 61143, seen here in steam on shed.*

The 'B1' had been officially withdrawn, from Immingham MPD (40B), the previous December, but the facts tell otherwise. The Austerity was itself withdrawn two months later, from Frodingham MPD (36C).

One of the most important freight centres in the country, March shed was host to a stud of freight locomotives over the years.

CONTENTS

Opposite *Fellow commuters were not much amused by my attempts to photograph the steam-hauled westbound morning freight from the open window of the 2-BIL unit on which I travelled from Sunningdale to Waterloo. The passing-place could be anywhere 'twixt Virginia Water and Feltham west yard, which joined the SR Reading line immediately to the east of Feltham Station, at which our train did not stop. On 2 July 1964, Maunsell 'S15' 4-6-0 No 30840 stood at the head of the freight, awaiting the road. Without the benefit to today's fast colour film, photography from passing trains was almost inevitably imperfect...*

INTRODUCTION

Blank stare — the start of yet another book, for yet another publisher. Naturally it must be different from any railway book yet published. Yet how can this be done? Perhaps a public soliloquy will entertain, or at least hold the interest of the reader, whilst finding an answer to satisfy myself and Patrick Stephens. A process of elimination aligned to the available features might help in the process.

This is not to be a technical or mechanical book, but it needs to contain an element of history and geography: in schools terms, 'A' Side, not 'B' Side. P.F. Saunders, not V.T. (only Old Uppinghamians will comprehend this bit, but it helps me). The market demands steam, steam and yet more steam, preferably in colour and certainly not previously published, yet supply is satiated with purely pictorial books. Nostalgia is an important, indeed a vital, component. Maps, particularly old railway-orientated maps, add spice, and colour too, if that can be arranged. In marketing terms, my book will aim to familiarize the reader with the subject, perhaps enabling him or her personally to enjoy today the experience I enjoyed when taking the photographs. Already, then, a pattern begins to emerge: the railway.

What motivated the early railway pioneers? Wealth and power, of course, had their part to play. Yet there was more, surely much more than the goal of mere material success. The spirit of adventure sparked off a revolution in travel, in social, as well as in physical, movement. Is it possible today to recreate that spirit of adventure, on the line — as it were — of the old trackbed? By rail, on foot, sadly by car we can explore; but imagination is the vital ingredient if we are able fully to appreciate those railway destinations of yesteryear.

By now you may or may not still be with me in my meditatory meanderings; but as was my hope, the writing of these words begins to clear my mind, and enables me to see, albeit dimly yet, the format of this book for which I search. We need, you and I, a shared experience. Come with me, then — let us together cover the tracks that I have covered.

In the railway's early days, the gazeteer was an essential component of the means by which the railway companies tried to seduce the prospective traveller. What has happened to that relationship between

Opposite *The Urie 'S15' 4-6-0s were amongst the last pre-grouping locomotives of this wheel arrangement to see active service on BR in the 1960s. No 30499 can be seen, at Waterloo on 21 August 1963, on page 22. Some 17 years later, on 4 July 1980, having languished at Woodham's, Barry, for 16 years since withdrawal, from Feltham in 1964, she prepares to face the future in preservation: one of the 'Barry escapees', whose tales have been told many a time and oft.*

Overleaf *Sonning Cutting, Mecca for steam: GWR 'Castle' Class 4-6-0 No 5014 Goodrich Castle heads a van train on the up slow line on 15 February 1964. The track nearest the camera is the down fast, and the distant glow of a single amber is just visible through the murky winter gloom. The cold air and dull light highlight the smoke effects of a real, not a contrived, railway scene. Note the GWR a.w.s. ramp on the up line. Goodrich Castle, built in 1932, was withdrawn in February 1965 from Tyseley, and cut up at Cashmores, Great Bridge, in May of that year.*

travel provider and travellers, these last 150 years? It is quite simple really: travel, which used to be a pleasure, has now become a chore. Travel, which used to be an adventure, has become a bore. Where there was a steam engine, a railway manned by people, individuals of character, each secure in his own community or in his own company, what have we now? We have anonymity. The engine driver and his fireman were *real* people; we often spoke to them before and after the journey. Who speaks to a bus-driver in his cocooned cab, or even to the train driver of today, clocking off before we reach the platform end?

How proud were our forebears to live in Great Western country. This statement needs no amplification. Yet who, with pride, proclaims 'I live in Wilts and Dorset country' or 'in Midland Red country'? And what about the architecture, the infrastructure; bridges, viaducts, tunnels across, over and under the natural hills and vales, nooks and crannies, rivers and streams — blending with the landscape, not blemishing it. Not only road, but air travel too, demeans the sheer pleasure of travel for travel's sake; if 'twere not so, why would private capital be available for a Channel Tunnel, so that a journey from London to Paris or Brussels may perhaps once again become a civilized means of inter-city communication? And whilst, for some, aircraft as such might be an attraction, who ever found a runway, a customs hall, an airport itself but a part of a means of travel, rather than a cathedral to a journey. How do you rate Old Oak Common engine shed with, shall we say, Victoria Coach Station or a British Airways hangar at Heathrow? Merely to ask the question is to answer it.

So far, perhaps, so good. But what about the call for 'something new'. There are books aplenty now about railway architecture and old buildings, and indeed about the remnants of departed lines with their slowly but steadily disappearing signs and sites across the landscape and in our cities and towns, large and small. What can I add to this? Having progressed thus far, thoughts are born and ripen. What of those colour photographs of steam, still alive and working in those final years from 1962 to 1968, when my camera was aimed at recording the end of the steam era in Britain? One thinks of Bristol and that magnificent Brunel train-shed. My good fortune as a Trustee of the Brunel Engineering Centre Trust has enabled me to trace the rebirth, from car-park dereliction to former glory, of this outstanding building. Indeed, one of my first colour photographs of steam, taken on 26 January 1963, was of a Bristol to Newcastle train about to depart thence.

Then there is Yeovil, where once one saw and photographed panting pannier-tanks in the Town Station, and watched the smoke rise from locomotives on Yeovil Town Shed (72C) against the green backdrop of the hill behind; now the most dreary, boring and featureless manifestation of modern life — the supermarket car-park.

Happily, much of our forebears' works remains and many still serve the rail passenger. Indeed on the Fort William to Mallaig line steam

has returned to grace the viaducts of this most wonderful of lines. Thanks to the heroic and patient work of the Steam Locomotives Operators Association (SLOA), it is again possible to see main-line steam on BR tracks, albeit bearing little resemblance to its forebears in the dying days of working steam, when visible paintwork was enough to enquire the reason for an appearance of cleanliness. The disappearance of the numerous appurtenances of the steam railway era, from the grandiose to the quaint — semaphore signals, water-troughs, signal-boxes, to name but three — are part of the disappeared magic that, for me, can never be reclaimed. Yet on the magnificent line to Mallaig even diesel trains enhance the landscape, be it only to emphasize their puny paltriness.

Somehow, dirt and grime, ancient buildings, and even that air of melancholia are a part of the pain and the pangs of a departed time. Thus one allows one's maudlin imagination to provide the warm glow of remembrance that is created by strolling through the weed-strewn tracks of Woodhams' scrapyard at Barry, or even rambling through the thorns and bracken of long-lifted track — even on lines where one never oneself saw the living railway.

What then of the preservation scene? My personal thoughts are hinted at by what I have already written. For me, solitude is an absolutely essential prerequisite for the enjoyment of steam nostalgia. Milling crowds, bad-mannered photographers, bawling children — all this and gleaming engines the like of which I knew not in the 'sixties are a monumental disincentive to the enjoyment of a scene, of an

BR Standard '5' 4-6-0 No 73016 trundles a freight down the LSWR main line, at the point where it crosses the SER Guildford-Reading line, on 15 February 1964. No electrification in sight, telegraph poles, winter gloom; and the type of freight traffic that BR's policy surrendered to the road transport industry. Incidentally, I wonder why that battered, rusting 'conductor rail' sign sits beside a line that, at that date, had never seen an electric train?

The Bluebell's Adams 'Radial' 4-4-2T No 488 was in action for private filming and is seen here at Horsted Keynes in the absence of 'tourists', the only circumstances in which I can appreciate and enjoy preserved steam. This splendid old lady, born in March 1885, has had an extraordinary career, having been sold by the LSWR to the Ministry of Munitions in 1917. Sold on to the East Kent Railway, in 1946 she was purchased at a cost of £120, derelict but intact, by the Southern Railway, successor to the LSWR, for service on the Lyme Regis branch. Finally condemned by BR in July 1961, she was purchased by the Bluebell in whose ownership she celebrated her centenary.

atmosphere that happily nonetheless attracts the tourists in their tens of thousands. 'Tourist' — that is what I am not and do not want to be, in relationship to the steam engine. Thus the *raison d'être* of the preserved railways, namely the creation of a public attraction with an ambience for 'the family' is by its very nature something that repels me, because my search is for the unattainable created through the use of imagination, rather than the attainable so superbly created by those very acts of preservation. Indeed, it is the very success of the preserved railways that keeps me away, and fortunate indeed it is for them that my behavioural pattern is the exception rather than the rule. For me, the best time to visit a preserved railway is when there is nobody else about, and one can wander quietly around, one's thoughts and memories stirred but not interrupted. How selfish I sound; but the last thing I would want to do would be to deter anyone from enjoying the prodigious feats of endurance, faith and energy that have created and sustained the preservation movement. My wish for solitude is a personal and private penchant.

Having mentioned not only the success of the preservation movement in attracting large numbers of visitors but also my predilection for their private quiet periods, it is only fair that mention be made of the

co-operation received from a number of these railways on occasions when a television company has wanted to film me at one or another. In particular my thanks are due to the Bluebell; to Steamtown at Carnforth, the nearest one can get to the old shed atmosphere; to the Bristol Suburban Railway at Bitton, of which I am President and which might not have come into existence were it not for my criticism and doubtless annoyance of BR in my Bristol political incarnation; to the Whitehouse show at Tyseley; but perhaps most of all, to David Shepherd at Cranmore. David's East Somerset Railway superbly encapsulates the spirit of struggle against hostilities, vested interest and bureaucracy, and survival to success if not to total security (no such realm probably exists in the uncertain world of railway preservation, although the Severn Valley's combination of good men, good sense and business acumen probably comes nearest to that desirable destination). Of all the preserved lines, at only one have I ever encountered high-handed pomposity and hostility, but even my outspokenness precludes further comment in that direction. As mentioned, 'private' viewings and steamings have been my privilege at a number of these lines, and one looks back with affection and gratitude at their early years.

Mention of the 'real thing' reminds me sadly that parliamentary and constituency obligations have precluded my participation in many main-line steam events, but a footplate run on *King George V* from Chester to Shrewsbury was a never-to-be-forgotten experience in 1983. Yet if solitude is one's satisfaction, then opportunity abounds almost literally from Lands End to John o'Groats, and here let me spend a moment in sharing with you the joys of discovery that lie at hand for any and every Briton. Indeed, the passage of time and the publication of ever more books about long-closed lines creates opportunities galore for exploration, investigation and satisfaction. One wonders how many teachers in our schools realize the potential that is represented for their charges in the disused railway lines that, sadly, cross every county in the land. What better way to teach today's youngsters about their own country than to take them on an exploratory ramble on the long-lifted tracks of a nearby line? Where shall we start?

At home in Todber, Dorset, we live but a few miles from that most evocative and truly wonderful of vanished railways, the Somerset & Dorset. Thanks to the work of that supreme artist/historian Ivo Peters, almost every conceivable location on the line has been faithfully photographed and recorded for posterity. Or has it? I cannot recall a picture of a train passing under the road-bridge at Hammoon. South-east from Templecombe, and before Blandford Forum, stretches a section of that line, including Sturminster Newton, that perhaps was, in S & D terms, almost neglected by the railway photographers. Criss-crossed by footpaths, the line today is clearly in evidence.

If the Somerset & Dorset, as a singular line, was well photographed

Overleaf *Awaiting their next turn of duty at Birkenhead shed, on a hot summer afternoon, 8 August 1965: Carlisle Kingmoor (12A) '9F' 2-10-0 No 92011; '8F' 2-8-0 No 48425; and, extreme left, Fairburn 2-6-4T No 42121. The thick, choking, acrid atmosphere of a large steam shed, on a hot, still summer day, was doubtless bad for the chest, but is great for the memory. Birkenhead shed, built jointly by the GWR and the LNWR in 1878, was a crumbling relic of the Victorian era by the mid '60s. The LMS 2-6-4 tanks worked the Birkenhead-Chester passenger trains, but it was freight work that sustained the shed throughout its life, which ended on 6 November 1967.*

and is well documented, let me at random pick out another stretch of adjacent rural railway, itself once designated as part of the main line of the Great Western Railway — the section between Yeovil and Athelney. 'Where?' you ask. 'Main line?' you query. Quite so. At first glance, this short stretch of Somerset railway line is probably thought of as a cross-country branch line connecting Yeovil and Taunton, as indeed in its latter years it was. But in the early 1920s, just prior to the grouping, it was an important artery for the GWR. Competing with the LSWR main line service from, say, Yeovil to Exeter, Plymouth and into Cornwall, one would take the 11.30 through train from Yeovil Pen Mill via Yeovil Town and Taunton, arriving at Plymouth (Millbay) at 4.22 pm, or the 2.25 pm from Pen Mill which arrived at Exeter St Davids at 4.30 pm and reached Plymouth North Road at 6.16 pm. Both trains called at Montacute, Martock and Langport West, thence on to the main line, calling at Athelney, Durston — the junction for Yeovil on the Taunton-Bristol line prior to the opening of the Castle Cary cut-off — and Taunton, thence fast to Exeter St Davids and the west. The London & South Western opposition offered the 11.37 from Yeovil Town, change at Yeovil Junction, thence depart at 11.53, with arrival at Plymouth Friary at 3.1 pm, or the 2.45 from Yeovil Town, change at Yeovil Junction with departure thence at 3.1, and arrival at Exeter Queen Street at 4.52. For travel further west, a change with some delay at Exeter was required; thus, in terms of passenger service and convenience for Yeovil customers, the long way round via Taunton, on a through train, was undoubtedly an attractive proposition. The GWR knew then the disincentives to travellers of having to change trains, as I am at present vainly trying to persuade British Rail of the consumer (today's word for customer) attraction of, say, a through rail link to Heathrow Airport from almost anywhere, if only they would 're-invent' the slip-coach. With the benefit of diesel or electric traction, powered slip-coach operation could open up a vast new potential network of 'through coach' services, the value of which the Great Western knew so well.

We have come a long way since my soliloquized question about the content and style of this book. Steam in colour, yes; some history and geography of lifted and of half-forgotten lines; early preserved railway scenes perhaps, on 'private' visits, but not too much, for books on our preserved railways are as rare as daisies on a spring lawn. The haunting memory of the dying shed, perhaps, or a 'then-and-now' sequence of an individual locomotive. The 'bridges, viaducts and tunnels' to which earlier reference was made. To what does it all amount? To clever critics, skilled photographers, learned historians, experienced engineers, elegant raconteurs — not much. To those who have no higher pretension than that of enthusiast, who seek not analysis but who unashamedly enjoy the pangs of nostalgia — come with me. Let us raise our glasses — 'The Railway'.

VALETE LONDINIUM

R ailway history, not surprisingly, starts at the beginning and ends at the finish. This is not an attempt to write the final chapter of such a tome, for my subject is confined to the last years of the steam locomotive *within* London's railway scene. This is no more than a vignette; nothing more learned than an invitation to accompany me around the engine-sheds and linesides of London, to join me in the reminiscence of retracing my steps in the metropolis, from my first railway photograph — of Fairburn LMS 2-6-4T No 42118 trundling through Kensington Olympia with a southbound freight in November 1962 — through the decline and demise of LNER, GWR, LMS and finally SR main-line sheds, to the last gasp of regular, normal, revenue-earning steam in London, as the fire died for the last time in the firebox of a pannier tank at London Transport's Lillie Bridge MPD. For London Transport, with its predecessors' pioneering electric railways, was the last of London's railways to eliminate steam, in 1971, some four years after the closure of the capital's last main-line steam depot, Nine Elms, on 9 July 1967. I was there, at the end.

Now that more than twenty years have elapsed since the last steam-hauled passenger train pulled remorselessly out of Waterloo, it is possible to discern the need to revise, slightly but perhaps not insignificantly, the presumptions upon which our memories are built, and the well-worn clichés that pedestrian scribblers like myself have churned out. 'Regular, normal, revenue-earning steam in London' — how does one define such a phrase? Regularly, steam-hauled trains leave Marylebone for Stratford-on-Avon. Business is booming. The threatened closure of Marylebone has evaporated. The October 1986 edition of *Steam Railway* headlined a news item 'BR doubles up on "Shakespeare" Steam', and as a separate item noted 'Christmas Steam for Marylebone'. In the same issue it was reported that Stanier 'Coronation' 'Pacific' No 46229 *Duchess of Hamilton* is to have her tender modified in order to increase its water capacity from 4000 to 5000 gallons. The reason for the undertaking of this substantial task is to facilitate longer running between stops from Marylebone to Stratford (and on other duties), clearly now expected to remain a feature of the railway scene in London.

Before returning to my coverage of the railway tracks around London

LNER 'A4' 4-6-2 No 4498 Sir Nigel Gresley enters Marylebone: is it 1958 or 1985? 'Regular steam working' has now returned to a London terminus.

in the final years of the steam era, it is worth mentioning the veteran Metropolitan Railway electric locomotive *Sarah Siddons*, and the projected conversion of Southall diesel depot for use by Flying Scotsman Enterprises (FSE) for the stabling, preparation, maintenance and overhaul of the main-line steam locomotives to be worked out of Marylebone. Thus at last, thanks to the initiative and determination of Bill McAlpine and his team, a 'southern comforter' may emerge to fill the gap of any active, permanent steam presence in London. If *Flying Scotsman*, *Clan Line*, *Sir Nigel Gresley* and *Sir Lamiel* obtain a firm foothold, it would only be a matter of time, hopefully, before public admission and Open Days were extended to make the most of Southall's main-line location. Indeed, travelling 'twixt Southall and Marylebone via West Ealing, Greenford and Northolt Junction would in itself be an attraction. We must ensure somehow a change in the curmudgeonly, not to say hostile, attitude to main-line steam that still represents the view of senior Western Region management. That, however, is another story. So, really, is *Sarah Siddons*, but in a chapter dealing with London's railway history and my own recording thereof, it seems legitimate to devote a couple of paragraphs to those distinctive Metropolitan Railway electric locomotives.

'Preservation' and 'electrification' seem somehow to be two inappropriate words to couple together. Electrification, as perceived, seems to imply modernity, yet it is over a century — in Brighton on 4 August 1883 on Magnus Volk's line from the Palace Pier to Black Rock — since the introduction of the first electric-powered public railway in Britain. Not surprisingly, steam locomotion in underground railways, whilst perhaps appealing nostalgically to today's enthusiasts, doubtless seemed less magical to London's late-Victorian travellers. The opening in 1900 of the Central London Railway between Shepherds Bush and Bank would hardly have been likely as a steam railway, however effective the condensing apparatus! By 1910, a number of London's railways amalgamated to form the London Electric Railway, and thus was established the pattern predictable since the opening in 1890 of the City & South London Railway, the first practical 'tube' (as opposed to mere 'underground') electric railway in the world.

The Metropolitan Railway, notwithstanding its name, spread more than 50 miles out beyond Baker Street. Familiar are the photographs of its far-flung, steam-operated extremities, the history of which is well enough recorded. Whilst steam's elimination from its nethermost regions was not seriously contemplated at the time, it was certainly that railway's ambition to eliminate steam from Baker Street. In 1906, experimental haulage of steam stock by electric locomotives 'twixt Baker Street and Wembley Park began. By 1 November of that year, all trains between these points became electrically hauled. By 1908, the change-over point from steam to electric haulage was extended from Wembley Park to Harrow-on-the-Hill. In 1925, Rickmansworth became the locomotive exchange point.

Those first electric locomotives ordered by the Metropolitan in 1906 were in two batches and were by no means identical. It was in 1922, however, that they ordered their third and final design. Although it was claimed that they were rebuilds of the original locomotives, it is now generally accepted that they were new, not least because the prototype of the twenty locomotives was actually a rebuild of one of the earlier locomotives and as such proved unsatisfactory. One of the new machines, No 15 *Wembley 1924* was displayed on the Metropolitan Railway's stand at the British Empire Exhibition at Wembley in 1925, whilst the remaining nineteen were named after famous people, real and fictitious, associated with the area served by the Metropolitan.

Strangely, the 1922 locomotives, with their curvaceous ends, look more antique than their predecessors, the shape of which more nearly resembles some of the smaller current BR diesel engines. No 12 *Sarah Siddons* is still active, alive and well and living at Ealing Common Depot. Accompanied by Kay Dixon, my long-suffering and increasingly railway-affected secretary, I spent an enjoyable couple of hours with her — or should it be with them! — on 13 October 1986. Naturally, London Regional Transport (LRT), successor to London Transport, to the London Passenger Transport Board and to the Metropolitan Railway, could not possibly be accused of the frivolity of preservation,

Overleaf *Urie 'S15' 4-6-0 No 30499, of 1920 vintage, together with two of Nine Elms' BR standard '3' 2-6-2Ts, Nos 82018/9, are amongst five steam engines visible at Waterloo on the evening of 21 August 1963. Note the porters keeping their barrows upright — how dull it all is now, compared to that day! My journey, from Waterloo to Yeovil Junction and Yeovil Town and return, ended with this shot; during the day I photographed thirteen different locomotive types. No 30499, for many years allocated to Feltham (70B), was withdrawn in January 1964, sent to Woodhams', Barry, for scrapping, survived, and is now restored by the Mid-Hants Railway, where she looks quite unlike any 'S15' in service on BR, but doubtless draws the tourists.*

Metropolitan Railway electric locomotive No 12 Sarah Siddons, *now London Regional Transport's mobile brake block test locomotive, stands at Ealing Common depot on 13 October 1986.*

so it is for functional not railway-fanatical reasons that *Sarah Siddons*, resplendent in her lined-out maroon livery, serves on the staff complement of LRT's Director of Mechanical Engineering, Mr Alan Waterman, as Brake Block Test Locomotive.

My brother, when first married, lived in Metroland, and thus I came to know, but sadly not to appreciate, the Bo-Bo locomotives when travelling out to see him. They continued in service on the through trains from Baker Street to Aylesbury as far as Rickmansworth until September 1961, steam haulage taking the trains on to Aylesbury, as they had done since time immemorial, until that date. Kay and I — if she disagrees with this she will doubtless refuse to type it! — enjoyed ourselves in *Sarah Siddons'* cab. Rattling along at a good lick, one was self-evidently in a vehicle from an earlier, more solid age. Experiencing the 'outdoor' lines of the underground system from the cab reminds one usefully of the importance of the railway in shaping the development of the metropolis. It also enables you to 'get away from it all', for the greenery of the embankments allied to the privacy of the railway environment separates and spares one from the madding crowd, the sprawling suburbs, the pushing and shoving of the modern world, where manners are forgotten symbols of a bygone era.

En route from Ealing Common to South Harrow on Piccadilly Line metals, we crossed the Great Western main line and the Great Central/ Great Western Joint. Some of the bridges under which we passed would probably qualify as architecturally meritorious when compared to the buildings beyond the railway in the areas through which we travelled. On arrival at South Harrow we stopped briefly in the station before crossing over on to the up line for the return to Ealing. This was a most enjoyable interlude, which serves as my opportunity to reminisce about my earlier memories of London's railways at the end of the steam era. Before finally leaving things electric, however, my comments earlier about the shape of the Metropolitan Bo-Bo electric locomotives calls to mind memories of Southern Region electric traction of my early memory, of odd-looking, tiny trains, of weird, lumpy trains, and of my own journeys into Victoria, where some of the electric trains had curved ends like *Sarah Siddons*, rather than the flatter-fronted PUL, PAN and LAV units on the Brighton-Victoria trains. From home in Hove, journeys by train to London were in fact journeys back to school, firstly to the evacuated Falconbury Prep School. I can extract from my memory departure on the 2.10 pm Paddington to Birkenhead train, and our school party alighting at Banbury. I seem to recall hearing that the school authorities tried but failed to persuade the GWR to stop the train at King's Sutton. How ancient I am getting, to be able to recall actually travelling on the Great Western Railway. My mind recalls carriage destination-boards: 'Banbury, Leamington, Birmingham, Wolverhampton, Shrewsbury, Chester, Birkenhead'.

After the war was over, and prep school returned to base near Bexhill, my rail journeys to London finished, to recommence in 1948 when Euston, not Paddington, was the cross-London destination from Victoria. Steamy, gloomy, sooty Euston seemed admirably to epitomize the mood of misery that prevailed on approaching the Uppingham School Special, for returning to boarding-school was not my favourite occupation. It was those journeys through the Southern's London suburbs that trigger the memory of those 'odd-looking tiny trains', the 'weird, lumpy trains' and those electric trains with curved ends.

The 'odd-looking tiny trains' were the two-car electric units with their distinctive cab roofs lower than the remainder of the unit's roof-line; in my ignorance I thought that the headcode '2' referred to the number of carriages. These two-car sets — eight in all — were in fact converted from the original 16 driving vehicles of the South London Line sets built in 1908/9, and it was the overhead electrical equipment originally fitted to these units that caused them to have a lowered roof over the cabs. Their conversion was undertaken in 1929, and the last of these vehicles, looking definitely antique by the early 1950s, was withdrawn in September 1954. I have an abiding memory of these trains, diminutive both in size and length, running into and out of Victoria's lengthy platforms.

The 'weird lumpy trains' comprised a four-car electric multiple unit, but with one of the cars completely ungainly and not matching the other three cars in style, size or shape. These units, designated 4-SUB, were in fact made up of one of the three-car suburban units augmented by the addition of a newly-constructed second-generation all-steel trailer. The first of these hybrid units entered revenue-earning service late in 1941. In fact, the ungainly odd-man-out coach in these four-car units that I can just remember were in due course to become the standard all-steel coaches in newly-built 4-SUB units, some of which, or at least some of the direct descendants of which, can still be seen in use on London suburban services. For full details of the '4-SUB saga', recommended reading is Colin Marsden's informative *Southern Electric Multiple-Units*, published in 1983.

From 'tiny trains' and 'weird lumpy trains', my third dim memory recalls those mysterious curved-ended electrics which one saw from the windows of my Brighton line PUL, PAN or LAV, but on which genteel travellers from the Sussex coast never travelled. They were 'inhabited', so I was once told by a vulgar fellow-traveller, by the 'great suburban unwashed' — a particularly inelegant phrase to describe passengers on what latter-day knowledge informs me now to have been the original electric trains built by the London & South Western Railway for its electrification of their suburban lines from Waterloo, fanning out to Wimbledon, Kingston, Hampton Court, Shepperton, Hounslow and Guildford. Built at Eastleigh, these distinctive, and to my eye elegant, units entered service on 25 October 1925. They were mainly converted from earlier steam-hauled suburban stock, but it was those bow-fronted ends that stuck in the mind of a railway-besotted youngster peering avidly through the window as the leisurely pace of railway activity across the fields of the Ouse Valley gave way to the frenetic flying junctions of Streatham.

'Twixt Streatham and Victoria, however, one glimpsed an even more mysterious world, thrust to the forefront of one's attention as the Brighton line's four tracks swung round the bend and under the bridge at Clapham Junction. Here was excitement indeed! Lines appeared from one knew not whence; tracks galore, carriage sidings, steam shunting — an endless whirl of excitement. To a mere adult, the phrase 'Clapham Junction' conveys but little interest; but to that young face glued to the window it meant a fleeting point of contact with the world that led to Waterloo, so one was reliably informed. Here were even odder-looking electric trains, notated in one's Ian Allan spotter's book as 4-COR, 4-BUF or yet 4-RES. With their central corridor gangway connection between each four-car unit, the front-end appearance of these sets was both odd and untidy in design, and scruffy in appearance. To the untidy front end was added a lop-sided appearance as a result of the side headcode. The driver's compartment thus occupied only half of the end section, with the through-corridor passenger space in the middle of the unit and the stencil headcode box blanking out the

other 'window'. My photograph of 4-COR unit No 3125 reproduced above may help to justify my rather unkind comments.

That photograph was taken on 23 March 1967, some thirty years after the introduction of the 4-COR units. It illustrates clearly the reason why the COR/BUF/RES trains became known as the 'Nelsons'; trains to Portsmouth, indicated by headcode 80, had a one-eyed appearance. By this date, the stencils had given way to roller-blinds, and these pre-war trains were approaching the end of their monopoly of the Portsmouth express services, if such an adjective is appropriate.

That colour photograph is, I think, the only one I ever took of main-line veteran electric units. By March 1967, my steam-photographic mission on the Southern was but four months away from its end; presumably that day, something jogged my memory of yesteryear and caused me to use a precious colour exposure on a mere electric train. For those of my generation, familiarity indeed brought contempt for the NOL, BIL, HAL, LAV, PUL and PAN units of my local environment. Thus they have all gone. I have never seen a colour photograph of a NOL — even black-and-white shots are scarce — yet they were the staple diet on the Brighton-West Worthing 'stoppers'. I am glad therefore to have captured 4-COR No 3125 for posterity. The BR blue livery did not suit the Southern EMUs, whilst the garish yellow 'full-frontal' merely accentuated the visual characteristics to which I referred earlier.

After displacement from the Waterloo-Portsmouth line, these distinctive SR motive power sets still served the railway system that bore them, carrying out their more humble duties on outer suburban services on both South Western and Central divisions of Southern Region.

'Nelson' on the wane: 4-COR EMU No 3125 heads an '80' headcode Waterloo-Portsmouth Harbour train past Nine Elms on 23 March 1967. These units looked far happier in Southern green, with, as I remember, gold numbers on the side, than in the turbid BR blue. Soon they were relegated to outer suburban and south coast semi-fast duties.

The old King's Cross, at the end of the steam era: an unusual photograph taken in March 1963, although no steam locomotive appears here. In fact I took this picture en route by foot from the station to Top Shed. With a few others on Agfa film featuring only diesels, I did not even bother to catalogue such photographs, and only now does their rarity and architectural, rather than motive power, detail merit a wider audience. The splendid signal box was demolished in 1977. Note the bull-head rail and wooden sleepers.

The Waterloo-Reading run was amongst their final regular rosterings; the last was withdrawn by September 1972, some thirty-five years old.

What romantic rambling this all is! Yet it is the romance of the railway that urges on my pencil, the sad romance that was personified by the decline and fall of steam in London, hence the title of this chapter. In that certain locations became the favoured haunts of contemporary railway photographers, London, as elsewhere in Britain, had its fair share of over-exposed, and equally its fair share of under-exposed, locations. My first photographs in central London were taken at King's Cross in November 1962. My very first LNER subject was 'A2/3' 4-6-2 No 60523 *Sun Castle*. Our acquaintance was brief; we met again in March 1963 when she was on the move, light engine, in that strange hinterland 'twixt King's Cross station and Top Shed, then finally at her last resting place, Peterborough New England shed, in the July of '63. With greased motion, *Sun Castle* stood proud but forlorn, one in a long line of dead engines awaiting her fate. She was cut up at Doncaster Works the following month, just one of that elegant band of 'Pacifics' that were synonymous with the LNER and King's Cross. King's Cross itself, at the end of steam and before refurbishment, retained its brooding atmosphere of Victorian opacity.

That Great Northern terminus in London was amongst the most heavily populated locations in the capital at which railway enthusiasts congregated. King's Cross Top Shed — 34A — has featured in numerous books, which is more than one can say of another London shed, a few miles distant in geography, but on another planet in terms of popularity and interest. For some reason 14A Cricklewood rarely features amongst the reminiscences or the pages of railway literature. Indeed, I cannot recall ever seeing a published colour photograph taken at the shed, which I visited on 6 April 1963 and again on 30 November, a year before it finally closed. Ere long it was demolished, the site cleared, and another site of railway archaeological interest was obliterated.

Why was Cricklewood shed so neglected? Was there a 'Cricklewood Factor'? Perhaps it is part of the saga of the 1923 Grouping, which created the Big Four railway companies. Of these, the LMS had the most painful birth. The intensive rivalry between its two largest pre-grouping constituent companies, the London & North Western and the Midland Railway, saw the latter emerge, surprisingly, as the 'brand leader' in terms of design, management and operation, although the LNWR still, in the minds of the railway world, remained the Premier Line. Euston rather than St Pancras was — and indeed still is — the senior terminus. Thus, in terms of 'railway appeal' the LNWR's London sheds at Camden and Willesden attracted much more interest amongst enthusiasts and photographers than the Midland's depots at Cricklewood and Kentish Town.

Cricklewood shed was nevertheless an important and substantial depot, albeit opened after Kentish Town. The relationship between the two sheds was close, but I never visited Kentish Town, although the opening sentence in Chris Hawkins and George Reeve's Volume Two of *LMS Engine Sheds* says of it that 'Kentish town was the Midland's London depot and opened along with the extension to the capital in 1867/8'. Cricklewood was thus born in the shadow of the Midland Railway's original London shed, a fact which doubtless helps to account for its seeming anonymity. An equally potent reason for its comparative failure to attract attention is its role — certainly in its early years — as a freight locomotive depot, linked inextricably with the Midland's huge coal traffic from Toton. Thus we can piece together the varied reasons accounting for the 'Cricklewood Factor', not least of which was the fact that Derby, rather than London, was the heart of the Midland Railway. London never appeared on the MR's coat of arms, that honour being shared by Brimingham, Bristol, Leicester, Lincoln and Leeds, as well, of course, as Derby.

When the Midland's tracks reached the capital it was by what the railway world knew as their 'London Extension'. Cricklewood — in the early years called Childs Hill — was out in the country and, as already mentioned, it was at Kentish Town that the company's first engine shed was located. Cricklewood shed itself was still called Childs Hill well into the early years of this century; indeed, 'Hendon' was

Overleaf *Green-liveried 'Coronation' 'Pacific' No 46239* City of Chester *simmers gently inside Camden shed on 28 April 1963, whilst another of Stanier's masterpieces stands behind. Camden shed, providing motive power over the years for the main express services from Euston on the West Coast Main Line, maintained a stud of LNWR/LMS/BR top-link locomotives and crews until the end of steam. None better combined speed, style, grace and reliability than Stanier's enlargement of his 'Princess Royal' Class, the magnificent 'Coronation' 'Pacifics', introduced in 1937.*

By the summer of 1963, the dreaded diesels would take over all the principal express working between Euston and Glasgow and the 'Coronations' would ere long be gone forever, as would the shed itself, which closed on 3 January 1966.

the original nomenclature given to the depot which ultimately, after Childs Hill and steady and extensive enlargement and development, became 14A Cricklewood in LMS days in 1935.

The inter-relationship of Cricklewood and Kentish Town sheds had a degree of social 'railway snobbishness' about it. Despite becoming the Midland Division's London 'concentration' depot, the former remained the unfashionable freight depot, whilst at Kentish Town was allocated the larger express passenger motive power, the 4-6-0s rather than the 'Pacifics' of the LNWR line — a reminder again of the 'minor' role of St Pancras as compared to Euston. Passenger services from St Pancras were dieselized (ugly word, ugly deed) in 1963, and some of the Kentish Town locomotives found their way to Cricklewood.

My two visits to Cricklewood Shed in 1963 yielded three 'Jubilee' 4-6-0s:

45561	*Saskatchewan*	Allocated Derby	(Withdrawn 5/65)
45653	*Barham*	Allocated Saltley	(Withdrawn 9/64)
45739	*Ulster*	Allocated Leeds Holbeck	(Withdrawn 1/67)

Re-covering those tracks to Cricklewood has rekindled memories of what appears to have been one of London's least-visited sheds, yet

Without access to the relevant working timetable, I know not the turn allocated to Holbeck 'Jubilee' 4-6-0 No 45739 Ulster, *seen here on shed at Cricklewood on 6 April 1963. I have not seen another published colour photograph taken at Cricklewood.*

Presumably the bases of the lighting-poles were painted white to enable shed staff to avoid walking into them at night. Ulster *was withdrawn in January 1967 and scrapped at Drapers, Hull, in June of that year. She was one of the last few 'Jubilees' to survive.*

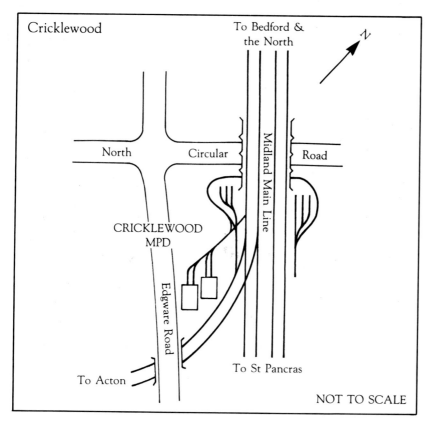

Cricklewood

To Bedford &
the North

N

North   Circular   Road

Midland Main Line

CRICKLEWOOD
MPD

Edgware Road

To Acton

To St Pancras

NOT TO SCALE

it was in fact one of the more easily accessible, being located at Staples Corner, the meeting points of the North Circular Road and the Edgware Road. The number 16 bus stopped almost outside the shed entrance.

Amongst the unusual features of the layout was a huge pear-shaped turning circle, running out behind the Shed, momentarily alongside Edgware Road then, like a giant model railway, plunging under the main line at the bridge which carried that line over the North Circular Road. The tiny corner of railway property, beyond the fence at the south-eastern corner of the Staples Corner road junction, was a private place which remained a minute rural backwater surrounded by the hubbub of road and rail movement. As the day of the diesel saw the sunset of steam, a new diesel depot opened on the east side of the main line opposite the declining steam depot. The diesel depot became 14A on 9 September 1963, when the steam shed, now showing signs of dereliction, became 14B 'Cricklewood West'. A handful of 'Black Fives', '8F's and '9F's found temporary refuge in the shed's hospitality into 1964, but ere the year was out steam had been banished forever. Who now remembers Cricklewood Shed?

The trouble with writing a chapter such as this is not where to start

Overleaf *Of all the London sheds, Old Oak Common with its four interconnected roundhouses had incomparably the most imperial atmosphere. Steam is in its final year here, as '28xx' 2-8-0 No 3849, with Croes Newydd (6C) shedplate, keeps company with one of the rapidly-dwindling band of my favourite class, No 7022 Hereford Castle, one of the BR-built engines. It is 23 January 1965, and the 'Castle' has a makeshift number-plate, whilst her shedplate has already gone, either to a bounty-hunter or into the safe keeping of Old Oak Common's staff. She and her companion are in the state of filthy neglect that so defaced the last surviving GWR engines in service on Western Region, but there appears to be the remains of white paint on Hereford Castle's buffers, perhaps indicating special use some weeks previously. She was one of the last 'Castles' to survive, being withdrawn from Gloucester (Horton Road) in June 1965.*

but how to stop; not what to insert, but what to omit. Top Shed, Camden, Nine Elms, Old Oak Common — they are, or were, the aristocrats of the steam era. The freight sheds were neglected; even towards the end of steam Feltham seemed rarely to attract much interest from the railway-photographic fraternity, and my friendship with Shedmaster Ted Richardson became a dual delight, both for his company and his endless patience with my interminable visits to his depot. To write a thesis on each London Shed would be beyond the scope of this chapter or this book; in any case, I am not restricting myself to engine sheds.

One obvious source of photographic potential was where railway lines crossed one another. London at one time must have contained untold gems. Indeed, my jaunt with *Sarah Siddons* took me across a

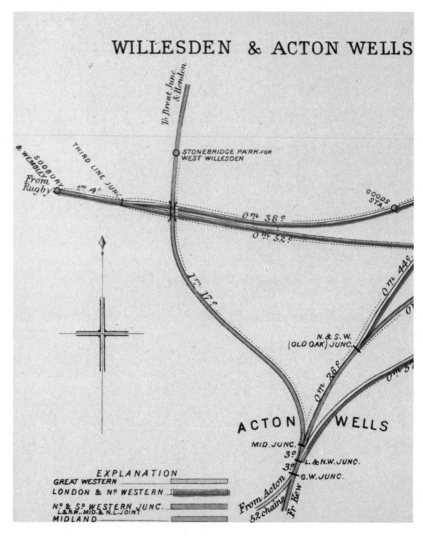

Bridge photography in the pre-grouping era, with a long lens and fast colour film, would have presented splendid opportunities! Such a location would have been here, where the Midland's link line from Acton Wells to its main line at Brent, crossed the LNWR main line from Euston, at the location illustrated (above right) some seventy-seven years after the publication date of this map.

couple of candidate bridges which never caught my attention in the steam era. Two such locations, however, had attracted me: the point just north-west of Willesden Junction where the Midland Railway's line from Acton Wells Junction to its own main line at Cricklewood and Brent crossed the LNWR main line from Euston; and at Wembley, where the Great Central crossed the LNWR line. Anyone fortunate enough to possess a copy of a pre-grouping Railway Clearing House map of 'London and its Environs', and who had the wit, the time, the camera and the enthusiasm, could have satisfied an insatiable appetite for steam photography any time in the first half of this century. Few so did. By the time the idea occured to me it was almost too late, and in truth the discovery of such potential goldmines yielded comparatively little. Of the two locations mentioned above, I can recall a southbound freight on the LNWR up slow main line trundling under the GCR overbridge on the day of the England v Scotland football match, 6 April 1963. My 'pitch' at Wembley that day has surely provided me with more lasting and more worthwhile memories, including a number of 'Britannia'-hauled football specials. I can even now recall the billowing smoke from Crewe North 'Black Five' No 45250 at the head of the freight, which included some interesting military hardware. It was the likelihood of finding steam-hauled specials that

Late in the day — 23 January 1965 — for LMS London steam, '3F' 0-6-0T No 47435 trundles a rake of wagons across the bridge over the main line from Euston at the location shown in the 1888 map (left). Electrification work is in evidence on the LNWR line, and the fireman watches the passage of a train heading for Euston on the line below him. The style — if that be the word — of the engine makes it hard to believe that this scene was photographed only just over twenty-three years before publication of this book.

Previous page *Feltham shed
was a frequent destination for
me, not least because of my
friendship with shed master Ted
Richardson. Here, on 23 January
1965, Eastleigh (70D) BR
Standard '4' 4-6-0 No 75074
stands over the ashpit and enjoys
the bright winter sunshine. The
comparatively modern shed and
adjacent marshalling and hump
yard were reduced to rubble and
dereliction — an appalling sight
for those who knew the place in
steam days.*

*The Standard '4' 4-6-0 was
designed at Brighton and
introduced in 1951. Designated
for 'light passenger and general
duties', they were a typical
product of the final flowering of
BR steam design — all-purpose,
unexciting and visually 'over-
exposed' for ease of maintenance.
This is one of the class to be
fitted with double blastpipe and
chimney; it says something for the
locomotive's appearance that this
barely affected their aesthetic
appeal, when it had destroyed
the appearance of a 'Castle'.*

*The first of the class was
withdrawn in 1964, scandalously
highlighting the waste of
resources epitomized by the
eclipse of steam. No 75074, a
Southern engine, was withdrawn
at the end of steam on the region
in July 1967.*

*Nine Elms Standard '3' 2-6-2T
No 82028 stands on the ashpit
behind No 75074, whilst a
Standard '4' 2-6-4T is visible
beside Feltham shed wall on the
left of the picture. The '3' was
transferred to the Southern
Region from York (50A) in
September 1963.*

attracted me to Wembley that day, and although the diet at this date was fairly thin, it sustained me, by that bridge, for some hours.

The other bridge mentioned above, namely the Midland overbridge just north-west of Willesden Junction, was a destination reached as a result of a 'controlled trespass'; an extension of my precious Willesden and Old Oak shed-passes on to adjacent railway property. It was — and still is — surprising how far enthusiasm causes one to wander. The extent of railway property encompassing Willesden shed, Brent sidings and beyond covers a substantial distance; yet on this particular January day my wandering took me from Old Oak Common shed, up and along the former MR line, in search of steam to add to my captures that day. At 81A, at the beginning of Old Oak Common's last year of steam, I had still been fortunate enough to photograph a 'Castle', a 'Hall', a '28xx' 2-8-0 plus '94xx' and '57xx' pannier tanks. Eventually I reached the bridge over the line from Euston and to my delight was greeted by a clanking LMS '3F' 0-6-0, No 47435. The locomotive was filthy, bereft of paint and without a shedplate. As I hastily photographed the engine at the head of its rake of empty wagons, an up van train ran past on the main line under the bridge, catching the attention of the '3F's' driver.

Writing these words, as I re-cover my tracks, it is twenty-two years to the day since that scene was captured in the lens of my trusty Voigtlander on 23 January 1965. Examining the transparency, the wisp of steam at the safety-valves seems the only indication that No 47435 is still alive, rather than a scrapped engine, so wretched is its condition. Wretched, yet utterly representative of the state of most of the contemporary steam stock still in BR revenue-earning service. These are the scenes that preservation cannot recapture, no matter how hard one tries. Amongst the features visible on close and detailed scrutiny of the picture (see page 37) are the crude brick steps up to the narrow walkway ledge over the bridge, semaphore signals in the background, and the masts for the wires of the West Coast main line electrification.

The joy of scribbling reminiscences such as this is the chance that it has provided to study the decline and fall of locomotives one photographed long ago. The railway enthusiast fraternity owes a consummate debt to Peter Hands for his painstaking research into the final years of thousands of individual locomotives. Thanks to his series *What Happened to Steam* I learn, all these years later, that No 47435 was transferred to Derby (16C) in December 1964; or was it? If you recall, I wrote earlier of the demise of steam at Cricklewood — 'ere the year was out, steam had been banished for ever'. Officially, indeed, steam *was* banished from Cricklewood Shed in December 1964, and according to Peter Hands, 47435, for years a Cricklewood engine, was transferred away to Derby that month. Yet there was I, on the bridge carrying the Midland line from Cricklewood, photographing 47435 on 23 January 1965. Had she really come down from Derby at the head of a rake of wagons? It seems most unlikely. Probably this errant Jinty hung on in the London area, on Midland tracks, eking out an existence, like some squatter, unwilling to face expulsion. Does anyone know the facts? Maybe somebody, somewhere, has a record, perhaps even of that train I photographed.

Presumably 47435 did make it to Derby for a few months in 1965. However, according to Peter Hands she was transferred to Wolverton Works in September that year, whence she was finally withdrawn, and scrapped soon after, in October 1966. Thus is illustrated the endless fascination of the life story of an engine, even an engine as humble and workaday as an LMS '3F' 0-6-0T.

Covering my tracks in search of steam in the metropolis had, by this time, become a very restricted occupation. According to my records, after that day to which I have just referred my metropolitan shed photography comprised visits to Feltham and Southall on 6 June 1965, and a number of visits to Nine Elms up until that dread day, 9 July 1967, the last day of working steam at an engine shed in the capital.

Feltham and Southall, rather like Cricklewood, never attracted the searchlight of glamour reserved for the sheds to which the main passenger engines were assigned. Southall has already attracted attention in this chapter and happily has clung to life and may now, well over twenty years since it hosted its last steam engine, provide facilities for engines of such distinction as its former inhabitants never knew as shedmates.

For Feltham, however, the railway link remained as but an entry in the asset ledger of the British Rail Property Board. Always a freight shed, the presence there even of a Bulleid 'Pacific' was noteworthy. Yet let it never be presumed that it was only the passenger classes that created interest or merited attention. Indeed, Feltham could offer more variety, late into the twilight of the steam era, than many a more famous or illustrious shed. My first six photographs there, on 11 May 1963, were:

LSWR 'M7' 0-4-4T No 30032	Maunsell 'Q' 0-6-0 No 30548
LSWR Urie 'S15' 4-6-0 No 30503	Maunsell 'W' 2-6-4T No 31917
LSWR Urie 'H16' 4-6-2T No 30518	Bulleid 'Q1' 0-6-0 No 33038

For sheer variety of interest in speciality classes, I doubt that any other London shed could have competed.

Feltham was a workplace of workhorse locomotives. Returning there in 1982, fifteen years after the shed closed, was heartbreaking. Dereliction and decay were all around; no steam, no life, seemingly no hope. All that was left were my abiding memories.

HIGHBRIDGE

It seems beyond my ability to write a railway book without a mention of this Somerset town. Should the temptation so to do have exceeded the merest flicker, then such thoughts were quickly and finally eradicated by the recent publication by Patrick Stephens Limited of an outstanding book entitled *The Somerset and Dorset Then and Now*. Utilizing many photographs from the incomparable camerawork of Ivo Peters and Derek Cross, its author Mac Hawkins has created a masterly memorial, a work both of reference and of nostalgia. Indeed, my first knowledge of the book was imparted to me by Ivo Peters himself, to whom I paid homage on a visit to his Bath home in June 1986, whilst my friendship with Derek Cross enabled me to enjoy the inestimable benefits of his editing of some of my own literary efforts.

My first encounter with Highbridge's railway heritage stemmed from my marriage to a girl whose school journeys in the 1950s took her by train from the family home in Burnham-on-Sea, by way of Highbridge, Evercreech Junction and Templecombe to Sherborne, although little perhaps did she then appreciate the significance of the Somerset & Dorset Joint Railway. However, by 1962 Jane herself propelled me into the act of photographing steam's declining years. A visit to her family home just after I had commenced my camerawork resulted in my obtaining, blissfully ignorant of their signficance, quite a number of now-irreplaceable shots of steam on the S & D at Highbridge; indeed, one or two photographs of steam involved movements from the S & D on to Great Western tracks at Highbridge. Thus is the temptation, fed by family, prodded by Peters and Cross, finally proven irresistable by Mac Hawkins and PSL.

Originality, not plagiarism, is not merely an asset; for me it is a matter simply of self-respect. The Peters and Cross photo-memorials to the S & D have, and will forever continue to have, their rightful place in the hall of fame. Mac Hawkins, by diligence and determination, has created an eminently worthwhile book. My only contribution, albeit puny, is to compare the changing landscape from 1962 over the quarter-century to 1987 through my own lenses. By chance, in sketching out the notional chapter headings for this book, there appeared a chapter entitled 'Highbridge to Hammoon'. Yet, just south of the hamlet of that name, the lane which we now use regularly en route to home in Dorset crosses the trackbed of the S & D. About a mile north-west of Shillingstone the line bore away — bears away, for surely it is immortal? — towards Sturminster Newton and, in a short cutting, ran under the Hammoon road. That no mention of this isolated place appears in print is no criticism, for to cover literally every inch of the 71½ miles of S & D 'twixt Bath and Bournemouth would be well nigh impossible. Yet Mac Hawkins has undoubtedly covered the line in detail with his *Then and Now*, so this chapter, like so much of our railway system, has been truncated. The points of direct contact between the S & D and other railways have mostly been obliterated from the railway map. With the honourable exception of the recently re-opened Southern stations at Templecombe, Highbridge alone remains rail-connected, at a point immediately adjacent to where passengers joined or alighted from Somerset & Dorset trains.

Students of British history from the inception of the industrial revolution cannot possibly fulfil their task adequately without some study and knowledge of the impact of the railway upon our country. That remains true today. Indeed, the understandable concern expressed in Swindon about the impact of the recent closure of the railway works upon employment and the welfare of the town highlights the pressure wrought by technological change upon seemingly settled circumstances. In truth, however, the effect on Swindon was minor indeed when compared to the effect upon Highbridge of the closure of the S & D locomotive works in 1930. To separate the story of Highbridge from that of the railway itself is illogical save only in the context of a short chapter related to my personal photography. In any case, the history of the line has been recounted frequently, and indeed extremely well,

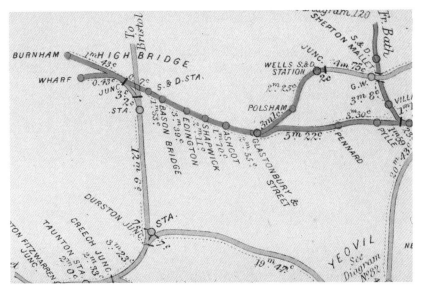

The Highbridge area in 1888: yellow is GWR, orange is S & D. Is it meaningful that the artist of this map allows the S & D orange supremacy over GWR yellow at the infamous crossing, which is visible at ground level in the picture on page 48? The spur on to the Burnham branch actually ran off the GWR down line, via a diamond crossover on the up line under the road bridge (see again the picture on page 48). As can be seen from this map, Wells was another inhospitable meeting place between the S & D and its great enemy the GWR.

in numerous books and articles these last few years; to the enduring skill of Ivo Peters' camerawork may be added the memorable prose flowing from the pen of Robin Atthill.

Only comparatively recently has the phrase 'industrial archaeology' become the common coinage of the language. Presumably those of us who recorded the passing of the steam era were practitioners of the study of that subject, although the phrase implies inert objects rather than living beings as epitomized by the steam locomotive. We photographed the train, but all too few of us bothered deliberately to record for posterity the attendant paraphernalia of the railway scene: the signals, sheds, water columns and towers, brackets and standards, posts and poles and the endless variety of buildings to house the locomotives, trains, trucks, people and things of the railway world. Now we look back on our old photographs and search longingly for these artefacts. Happily, the technological advances in photographic reproduction facilitate both clarity and enlargement of elderly colour photographs.

Highbridge was indeed rich in such railway-related industrial archaeology, but a careful study of some of my photographs reveals mainly what I 'missed', rather than what I 'hit' by accident. The 1930 hammer-blow, when hundreds of people lost their jobs at a stroke, was called to mind by the sight, years later, of the buildings of Highbridge Locomotive Works, seen in the background, by sheer chance, of a handful of my photographs. More fortunate, for me, was the fact that one of my very first photographs, indeed my first interior 'shed shot', was taken inside the diminutive Highbridge MPD building. What I never bothered to record, through blissful ignorance, was the quite extensive maritime artefacts of the S & D, both at Highbridge and at Burnham-on-Sea. Indeed, the station at the original northern terminus of the line was not actually the northernmost point, that honour falling to the line laid on the pier and slipway from which, in August 1858, a Cardiff-based ship, the *Taliesin*, began a service between Burnham and the Welsh capital. Tide, silt and weather soon put paid to Burnham's maritime role, with the S & D services being transferred, by 1867, to Highbridge Wharf.

I suppose that Burnham slightly, but Highbridge greatly, epitomized two towns suffering from dashed expectations. Those pretentious posters of the twin-funnelled, two-masted paddle steamer *Sherbro*, the S & D's last steamer for the Burnham-Cardiff run, acquired in 1884, sported the splendid legend 'Shortest and Cheapest Route for Goods and Passengers to and from South Wales The South West of England Somersetshire Dorsetshire Southampton Bournemouth Poole Isle of Wight the Channel Islands and France via Southampton'. One needs to try to imagine the expectations aroused during the early years of railway development fully to appreciate the boundless dreams and schemes abounding in the heads and hearts of the men and women in those towns touched by the explosion of the railway age.

Opposite *Great Western interloper: Collett '2251' Class 0-6-0 No 2219 inside Highbridge Shed in December 1962.*

This is one of my first railway photographs, and is the only colour shot I have ever seen of the shed's interior. Note the 82G shedplate, the code for Templecombe, which was changed to 83G in October 1963. (Peter Hands in What Happened to Steam *records No 2219 as a Taunton (83B) engine.) Note also the pendant gas lamps.*

The fiercely loyal S & D men deeply resented the replacement of their Midland/LMS locomotives with alien GWR motive power. The exterior of the shed is visible in the background of the photograph on page 50.

Highbridge (East), as the S & D station was latterly known, had five platforms, two forming a bay, at one of which stands Templecombe's Ivatt 2-6-2T No 41214 with the 14.20 train to Templecombe on 20 February 1965 — note the 'mixed' stock. Nostalgia haunts the student of these photographs, with their reminders of forgotten details of the buildings of the railway at Highbridge. The missing arms of the signal (top left) tell their own tale, of the through lines to the Burnham branch, and the tortuous connection with the Great Western tracks (see the picture on page 48). The locomotive's chimney appears to have suffered internal damage to the rim. In the background, above the second coach, is the bridge carrying the B3139 road over the Great Western (formerly Bristol & Exeter) main line.

The S & D's intended role for Burnham was as the English maritime terminal for the cross-Bristol Channel packets to Cardiff. The tidal problems were but one of the reasons why these grand plans never really flourished; the service was abandoned about four years after the acquisition of the *Sherbro*, and in 1905 the S & D sought Parliamentary powers to sell or to abandon Burnham Pier. The rails on the pier, however, remained for many years, used for assisting in the launch of the lifeboat. Thus Burnham relapsed into a genteel resort, with its single cinema — The Ritz — and its most prestigious store, Cox & Cox, serving the needs of the local population: by the time of my first visit with Jane, Burnham and Berrow Golf Club had lifted its embargo on membership to those 'in trade'. Although the 1½ mile extension of the S & D from Highbridge to Burnham had, together with Wells and Bridgwater, lost its regular passenger service back in 1951, a stub of the line, together with the junction pointwork and the notorious crossing on the level with the GWR Bristol-Taunton main line at Highbridge, remained.

Highbridge, however, even in 1961, seemed to me a sad, melancholy and neglected place; a once-thriving town that had never really recovered from the closure of the S & D Works. Again, one needs to be able to take a step back in time to those early heady days of the Somerset Central Railway. It was in February 1862 that the first buildings of Highbridge Works, those for the repair of locomotives and rolling-stock, were brought into use. From small beginnings more land was acquired, more buildings erected, and the extent and scope of the works' capability was enlarged. Occupying a space approximately the shape of an isosceles triangle, with the River Brue bounding the long side of the triangle and the line to Evercreech on the other, the site eventually contained a complete range of shops for the rebuilding as well as the repair of locomotives and of passenger carriages and wagons. There was a foundry, erecting shop, spring shop, boiler shop, machine shop, paint shop, saw mill, stores and drawing office, not to mention, alongside and part of the same site, the running shed, carriage cleaning and testing shed, coal stack, turntable and other paraphernalia of the motive power depot. Historic accounts vary as to whether three small tank engines were built there, or whether one (0-4-2T No 25A) was built new and the other two (0-4-0Ts Nos 26A and 45A) were rebuilds; regardless of such detail, Highbridge Works was so dominant in this small Somerset town as was Consett's steelworks.

At the 1923 Grouping, the amicable partnership of the erstwhile London & South Western and Midland Railways was maintained by the SR and LMS. But at the end of that decade the national slump struck, and few places were dealt a more crippling blow than that which fell on Highbridge. The 'reforms' of 1930 were the first major changes

In the left foreground of this June 1980 picture stand the remains of Highbridge (East) up platform. The black bridge carrying the B3139 across the GW line survives. On the right is the temporary spur off the down GW main line, used to carry spoil from South Wales for M5 construction works. It too has long since gone, as have the telegraph-poles seen in the picture opposite.

Arguably the best-known level crossing on the British railway system: the unfriendly oblique meeting-point of two hostile systems, the S & DJR and the GWR at Highbridge. This crossing was immediately to the north of the GW station on the main line to Bristol — here disappearing into the distance. The S & D line, over which the milk-tank next to the engine is passing, is the erstwhile line to Burnham, reduced to a shunting stump at the date of this photograph, 28 July 1963. The engine is Templecombe's Ivatt '2MT' 2-6-2T No 41242. The road overbridge carries the B3139 and one of the road's signposts, indicating 'Burnham' and 'Highbridge', is now in our Dorset garden.

in S & D administration since 1891, and the most drastic since the LSWR/MR take-over of the line in 1875. It was in 1891 that the partner-owners decided that heavy locomotive repairs would be undertaken in Bristol and research in Derby, whilst ordinary loco repairs, and the full activity of the carriage and wagon depot, would be maintained at Highbridge; on the later date the guts were ripped out of the town. In that fateful year of 1930, the run-down of the works began in January; by May it was all over, and 68 years of pride, of individuality and of character were turned to dust. It was a shattering blow to the little town, and even in 1962 when I took my first railway photograph there, the sadness and depression seemed all-pervasive. At the time of the closure, many families moved away in search of railway work elsewhere; to Derby on the LMS, to Lancing on the SR, even to Swindon on the hated rival GWR. But unemployment hung like a cloud over Highbridge; rust and decay, loss of earning power, boarded-up shops... Unlike Consett or Corby, half a century later, no scheme was put in hand to help to revitalize and renew the town so dependent on one employer. Somehow, Somerset seemed set apart from those areas of Britain worst afflicted by industrial change.

If Highbridge never quite fulfilled the expectations aroused by the birth of the S & D, it could claim an important role on the system itself, long after the opening of the new line from Evercreech to Bath had relegated the Highbridge line to branch status — the Works saw to that. It was somewhat incongruous for a railway system to have its main Works near the end of a branch line — as though Swindon were at, say, Fairford. However, some of my photographs happily, albeit incidentally, record in the background that part of the S & D's 'industrial archaeology' that was still in use at Highbridge at the end of 1962 until final closure of the line in March 1966.

The feelings aroused by the line's closure have been recorded frequently and with deep feeling on many occasions by numerous people. Bitterness, betrayal, sadness, anger; yet from the moment that the Western Region effectively gained control of the S & D in 1958, foreboding was evident. With the publication of the Beeching Report in March 1963, a few weeks after my first photographs were taken at Highbridge, foreboding gave way to fear of the inevitable. I was a new boy to the line, as yet unaware of its very distinctive character. At Highbridge I talked to some of the long-serving railwaymen, and began

Seventeen years later, the bridge with its patches remains, and the fence off the end of the GW up platform has been repainted. No trace remains of the Somerset & Dorset line, the goods shed or the sidings visible in the photograph above left. Little boxes epitomize today's architecture, whilst in the distance the next bridge up the line towards Bristol and a thin factory chimney are about the only other constant features.

With an LMS engine in the foreground — Ivatt 2-6-2T No 41208 of 83G Templecombe — the numerous buildings of the works, shed, water-tower, together with the extensive track layout, points and signal rodding, and the guards vans on the right, Highbridge on 20 February 1965 still retains the timeless appearance of a busy railway centre. Straight ahead is the line to Bason Bridge and Evercreech Junction. A year later the S & D would close forever, the site would be cleared and the M5 motorway would cut a scar across the landscape. Just out of interest, compare the chimney of No 41208, seen here, with that of sister engine No 41214 on page 46.

to obtain a feel for the line, albeit at the truncated end of a withering branch of a dying trunk. For those dwindling numbers of the local citizenry of Burnham-on-Sea and Highbridge who travelled by train, it was on the GWR to Bristol or Taunton rather than the S & D to Evercreech or Templecombe to which people referred when, infrequently, they discussed rail travel.

Whilst even in the last few years of the Bath-Bournemouth main line motive-power innovations occurred, such as the introduction of '9F's on the line, the locomotive interest on 'The Branch' generated more aggravation than acclamation at Highbridge. As the older LMS locomotives were withdrawn, it was GWR engines that replaced them. Collett 0-6-0s appeared on the Highbridge-Evercreech trains, often in deplorable mechanical condition. Then, the final insult to the S & D man — pannier tanks appeared on the scene. Although for my part these locomotives seemed to blend quite well into the landscape, for railwaymen who for generations had worked with Midland machines the GWR engines represented the hated rival whose take-over of their railway was epitomized by Swindon motive power. It was as though the GWR and its BR successor would ensure the demise of the S & D by hauling it to its own funeral.

Winter sunshine in January 1963 illuminates the Highbridge water-tower, alongside which Ivatt 2-6-2T No 41304 awaits her next turn of duty, the Sunday milk train. Close scrutiny of the minutiae on and around the water-tower is rewarding.

At this date carrying an 82E Bristol Barrow Road shedplate, No 41304 was transferred away to Shrewsbury the following September. From thence she went to Bank Hall (Liverpool) and to Aintree in August 1965, from where she was finally withdrawn in November 1966. She was cut up at Cashmore's, Great Bridge, in March 1967 — a sad but inevitable end to an LMS engine once at home on the S & D, for she was allocated to 71J Highbridge — at that date safe as a Southern Region shed — from March 1957 to May 1959.

Collett '2251' Class 0-6-0 No 3210 of Templecombe sets off from Highbridge on the original S & D main line — 'The Branch' after the opening of the Bath line — with the 16.00 train to Wincanton on Saturday 18 August 1963. Ere long the S & D will have gone, and all trace of the railway obliterated as the M5 cuts a swathe, left to right across this picture, just beyond the shed building on the right. With its tall signals, telegraph poles and track towards Bason Bridge (see the map on page 43) disappearing across the Somerset levels, this picture surely epitomizes the sad, lonely end of this most distinctive of English cross-country railways.

The farce and tragedy of final closure are, as earlier stated, well enough documented for me to resist the temptation to relive the agony in words. The S & D had the last hollow laugh on the Western Region by preventing the region from achieving its wretched ambition to eliminate steam by the end of 1965; withdrawal of an anticipated replacement bus service saw the authorities forced to maintain a skeleton 'service' on the line into the first few weeks of 1966. On my final visit to Highbridge — when at that time I was still unaware of the real nature of the tragedy that my camera was recording — it was at least still an LMS locomotive, Ivatt 2-6-2T No 41208, that comprised my last steam photograph there.

This evocative place, of such fond memory to anyone who knew it in its S & D days, even in their decline, has drawn me back on several occasions; it is painful, really. Whilst the M5 motorway — I refuse to give this word a capital 'M' — has perhaps boosted Burnham, albeit turning it practically into a commuter point for Bristol, the new road seems to have brought little joy to Highbridge. Whilst the dreaded

A38 through Highbridge no longer creates suffocating traffic jams that clogged the little town from end to end on summer Saturdays, the motorway has been but one more factor in removing trade. Indeed, whilst it was being built a temporary rail spur was put in off the GWR down main line through the site of the former S & D station. The spur provided rail access for thousands of tons of ballast and slag required to build the M5 across the Somerset flatlands. The spur ran through the old station and, for all the world as though it were on its way to Bason Bridge, Edington Burtle, Ashcott and stations to Evercreech, ran on — but not far, not far at all. These trains climbed a specially-constructed temporary embankment whence they disgorged their loads over a screen and, via a run-round loop for the diesel locomotive, disappeared whence they had come. Thereafter the last rails at Highbridge S & D were lifted, the temporary Bailey Bridge put in for this work having already gone.

Long before the insulting finality of the use of S & D property to build a road, the station, signal boxes, signals, lamps, the very life, the existence of the Somerset & Dorset Joint Railway had been obliterated from the Highbridge scene. I was privileged to know it, at its end. It may be gone; its memory will never, never die.

Some 18 years later, the M5 is open: the temporary track seen here is the line used to convey spoil in connection with the motorway's construction. Even this temporary track is now a nearly forgotten memory.

TUNNEL VISION

This is a chapter based more on emotion than on engineering, more on fantasy than on fact, for surely of all the physical features of railway construction the tunnel is more surrounded by excitement of the emotions than is any other attribute of the work of the engineers. Indeed, it was whilst reading chapter XVI of Volume II of Smiles' *Lives of the Engineers* that my thoughts on the subject of tunnels were crystallized into this chapter. Furthermore, it was research for the chapter 'Last stronghold of steam' that led me to the section in that book relating to the Manchester & Leeds Railway, with its references to Summit Tunnel, that determined me in this direction.

Over the years, famous and infamous people have been associated with this area of the Pennines. One built a great hole under the moors; one stamped his personality on his constituency that included the moors; and two wrought vile deeds in the same neighbourhood. Some have featured in, or been featured in, heated Parliamentary exchanges. George Stephenson, accustomed to the bitterness, rivalry and enmity that surrounded the fiercely competitive early years of the railway builders, can have faced fewer more unpleasant situations than occurred when the Manchester & Leeds Bill was before the Committee of the House of Lords. Suddenly, Stephenson was accused of dishonesty in the representations he was making. His accuser, Lord Wharncliffe, happened to be a director of the rival Manchester & Sheffield line, to which reference is made in 'Last stronghold of steam' (page 173), and which itself pierced the Pennines through the Stygian gloom of Woodhead Tunnel. Accusing Stephenson and the promoters of the Manchester & Leeds of deception, Wharncliffe turned to Stephenson and, to his face, said 'I ask you, sir, do you call that conduct honest?' Stephenson, voice trembling with emotion, replied, 'Yes, my Lord, I do call it honest. And I will ask your Lordship, whom I served for many years as your enginewright at the Killingworth Collieries, did you ever know me to do anything that was not strictly honourable? You know what the collieries were when I went there, and you know where they were when I left them. Did you ever hear that I was found wanting when honest services were wanted, or when duty called me? Let your Lordship but fairly consider the circumstances of the case, and I feel persuaded you will admit that my conduct has been equally honest throughout in this matter.' Smiles then comments 'He then briefly but clearly stated the history of the application to Parliament for the Act, which was so satisfactory to the Committee that they passed the preamble of the Bill without further objection. Lord Wharncliffe requested that the committee would permit his observations, together with Mr Stephenson's reply to be erased from the record of the evidence, which, as an acknowledgement of his error, was permitted.' I cannot see Hansard allowing such tampering with the Official Report to be permitted nowadays.

Tunnels, by their nature dealing with darkness and the unknown, often generated rumours of disaster, some such rumours sadly being subsequently proven to be true. Relating to Summit Tunnel near Littleborough, however, rumours were spread around Manchester that, as completion approached, the tunnel had collapsed and buried many of the workmen. The rumour was based on a trivial accident to an invert. At the scene of the 'frightful accident' of Mancunian rumour, all that was visible was 'a certain unevenness of the ground, which had been forced up by the invert under it giving way; thus the ballast had been loosened, the drain running along the centre of the road had been displaced, and small pools of water stood about. But the whole of the walls and the roof were still as perfect as at any other part of the tunnel'. Further detail follows, confirming that 'not the slightest fracture or yielding could be detected'. Later that day, George Stephenson said 'I will stake my character, my head, if that tunnel ever give way, so as to cause danger to any of the public passing through it. Taking it as a whole, I don't think there is such another piece of work in the world. It is the greatest work that has yet been done of this kind, and there has been less repairing than is normal — though an engineer might well be beaten in his calculations, for he cannot beforehand see into those little fractured parts of the earth he may meet with.'

If Stephenson be accused of immodesty he cannot be charged with incompetence. This incident in the career of one of the world's greatest engineers seems well to illustrate the challenges accepted and overcome that so richly credit the early years of the Railway Age. How puny and pathetic seem the efforts of Stephenson's latter-day contemporaries of our present generation, with all their modern equipment and technology. Summit Tunnel involved a labour force of more than 1,000 men for nearly four years. In addition to excavating the arch out of solid rock, they used 23,000,000 bricks and 8,000 tons of cement in the building of the tunnel. Thirteen stationary engines and 100 horses were employed just in drawing the earth and stone out of the shafts. Phrases like 'industrial relations' or 'working conditions' were not invented. When in December 1984 there was an accident, explosion and fire in Summit Tunnel, the construction in which George Stephenson took such pride some century and a half earlier was shown to be well justified. As Keith Parry wrote in his booklet *Survivor*, which tells the tale of that awesome fire, 'How could the 140-year-old tunnel — even though it had been built by superb Victorian engineers — possibly survive the searing heat of a fire of this magnitude?' It did.

The Woodhead Tunnels, like Summit penetrating the Pennines, also combined prodigious feats of engineering with horrendous social problems. The work was hard and brutal, the circumstances uncertain and the atmosphere underground vile. During excavation and construction of the first bore, 32 workers were killed, 140 seriously injured, and many badly affected by the unhealthy atmosphere in that Stygian cavern. Whilst accidents caused fewer deaths in the digging, cutting and boring of the second tunnel, disease took a terrible toll. The navvies working in the bleak and barren landscape set up a ramshackle camp — an insanitary shanty-town. Cholera took hold in this gruesome place. Unknown, unremembered and unrecorded were many of the men who died; forty in one night alone.

At Kilsby was played out the greatest drama in the construction, in 1837-8, of the original London and Birmingham Railway. Roade, Tring and Blisworth cuttings had been overcome, not without considerable difficulty. But at Kilsby, south of Rugby, all the dangers facing the tunneller were present in abundance, with the indeterminable horror of treacherous springs presenting fearsome and unforeseeable hazards. As if the problems associated with pervasive water were not sufficient, the engineers came upon quicksands, themelves fed by underground streams from what transpired to be a subterranean lake. Nineteen months of seemingly endless toil were necessary before the sand was checked and controlled, by which time the original contractor on this section of the railway suffered a complete mental and physical breakdown, and died. George Stephenson's equally famous son Robert took over and completed Kilsby Tunnel, and indeed the line.

Summit, Woodhead and Kilsby Tunnels were, each one, epics in their own right. Why has not Cecil B. de Mille recreated the drama, uncertainty, excitement, intrigue and emotion involved therein? Yet these are but three tunnels. The tale of the Severn Tunnel and the constant battle against the waters is well enough documented. To list those tunnels which merit a chapter to themselves makes one realize how little notice has been taken, by all save a few *cognoscenti*, of such a fascinating subject. What of Blea Moor or Box; of Clayton or Catesby; of Knighton or Totley or Whiteball — the list is endless. So this brief soliloquy of lines subterranean must of necessity be but of personal predilection.

I cannot remember the first time I traversed — if that is the correct word — a main-line railway tunnel; indeed, my first train journey is lost in the mists of time, although Nanny said that by the age of three I had memorized every photograph in *The Wonder Book of Trains*. At

Catesby Tunnel: visible remains of the Great Central Railway on 18 August 1987. Note the date of construction boldly portrayed.

the outbreak of war we were taken — by car — to Cornwall. My evacuated Prep School was at Astrop Park, near King's Sutton. The family home by then was Hove, and train-spotting commenced chronologically hereabouts, so my first experience of passing through a tunnel would probably have been Cliftonville, nearby where we lived, or Patcham. Neither is remarkable, save only for the thought that urban tunnels seem quite unknown to those who *live* over or near them. That seems strange, somehow — as we shall see.

As my railway interest grew, shared to a lesser extent by my contemporary friends, I recall excursions by bicycle. On the LBSCR main line, the turrets of Clayton tunnel, encompassing and surrounding a seemingly-impenetrable black hole, still call to mind those mixed emotions of mystery, fear, anticipation and inquisitiveness that so impressed themselves on a boy's mind. Notwithstanding the electrification of the line — a certain deterrent against tunnel exploration —

the freight trains were still steam-hauled, and their engines' smoke would hang stickily around the tunnel mouth, often to be disturbed by the rushing emergence of a 6-PUL + 6-PAN Brighton-London 'fast' with headcode '4'. Such are the memories of youth. Patcham, Clayton, Quarry and, in those days, Coulsdon tunnels are remembered too, as on Friday nights we would pay 1/6d extra to travel Pullman Third-class, the pink table-lamps reflecting off the carriage windows as we sped southwards through the tunnels, weekly stipend in our pockets, opulence personified in our Pullman seats.

Whilst occasionally I envy those who carefully plan their lives, my experience is that haphazard progress along life's path often creates, through random chance, unexpected opportunities. Thus, my selected reading for a visit to Malaysia whilst writing this book provided snippets of information from Adrian Gray's *The London to Brighton Line 1841-1977*. In addition to Clayton and Patcham Tunnels, referred to above and which I traversed twice daily as a young commuter, there was the short tunnel immediately to the south of Haywards Heath station. Only now do I learn that it is known as Folly Tunnel. From Mr Gray's book comes the information that three men were killed during the latter stages of the tunnel's construction. Although it was incomplete, ballast trains were traversing it but the roof was so low that a 'rack and pinion' device was used to lower the chimneys of the engines as they ran through. On 2 January one driver failed to lower the chimney in time, and it brought the roof down, suffocating three men. A verdict of 'accidental death' was recorded with a forfeit of 1/- on the chimney.

Two other tunnels on the Brighton line, those at Balcombe and Merstham, were lighted with gas. In those early railway years, rail travel through tunnels aroused wild and oft-exacerbated fears. Some of my Parliamentary colleagues opposing the Channel Tunnel on spurious grounds would do well to read the Victorian railway writer, John Francis, who wrote 'The public could not or would not understand that it was as safe to travel in a dark tunnel as on a dark night'. It was said that the chill of a two-mile subterranean passage would deter any person of delicate health from even entering them. Anthony Carlisle asserted that 'tunnels would expose healthy people to cold, catarrhs, and consumption'. Contemporary fears were easily aroused about railway travel in general, and the passage through tunnels in particular. Some of the pessimists and purveyors of doom, with whom we are so plentifully supplied in Britain, predicted that passengers in steam-hauled trains would be burned alive in their carriages. *Plus ça change!*

If travel through tunnels was perfectly safe, living on top of one particular one, as we shall see, proved hazardous and indeed deadly, more than a century after Clayton Tunnel was opened. But it was the tunnel builders, rather than travellers, who were subjected to inhuman, outrageous and often fatal conditions. Indeed Clayton Tunnel itself claimed a victim in March 1840 when a navvy, whilst ascending one of the shafts, was 'dashed to pieces by the breaking of a rope, which appeared to have been designedly cut almost through'. Thus was the morbid event described by the *Brighton Gazette*, which attributed a 'mysterious air' to Clayton.

The tragedy above described was, of course, as nothing to the horrors of Woodhead, where the 1,500 or more navvies camped out on the bleak, desolate, gale-ravaged, rain-soaked Saddleworth Moor 1,500 feet above sea-level existed in unspeakable conditions. I have seen the grisly conditions in the Palestinian refugee camps — but the inhabitants there are victims of political and military aggression, not employees of a British engineer building a railway. It was the inhuman circumstances inflicted upon these exploited wretches that finally attracted Parliamentary attention, culminating in the enquiries of a Select committee set up in 1846 to investigate the 'condition of railway labourers'.

It was politics too that enabled me to obtain the picture below of an LBSCR train emerging from Clayton Tunnel, hauled by Class 'B4' 4-4-0 No 54. A luncheon invitation from the chairman of the

The story of how this picture was lent to me is recorded in the text. How splendidly the artist has caught the excitement of the emergence of LB & SCR 'B4' 4-4-0 No 54 Empress. The cottage above Clayton Tunnel's north portal cost £64 when built, the main line to Brighton opening in September 1841.

Highcliffe Branch of the Christchurch & East Dorset Conservative Association, Sid Keeling, led inevitably on to railways. My host, an ex-railwayman who joined the LMS in 1937 produced for my inspection a splendid collection of railway postcards. He kindly allowed me to borrow the one illustrated: it is postmarked Eastbourne and stamped 7.15 pm 29 March 1907. Such is the happy coincidence of writing railway books, and I could not resist looking into the history of that 'B4' No 54. Originally named *Empress*, this locomotive, so splendidly painted in that postcard, was renamed *Princess Royal* in August 1906. By melancholy chance she survived not only to become Southern Railway No 2054, but into BR days when the railways were nationalized in 1948. Although in poor mechanical condition No 2054 was never renumbered by BR and was in store in Eastbourne in 1949 when, to the consternation of the shed staff, written instructions were received on 13 December to send her to Brighton for duty on the Christmas parcels traffic. Together with sister engine No 2063, which had also been in store for over 3½ years, her tubes had been swept clean by the wind and rain of several winters. A telephone call to Brighton revealing the plight of this ancient lady, built in May 1900, caused this final call to duty to be rescinded. Left undisturbed, 2054 and sisters made their last journey, to Brighton for breaking up, in May 1951. Nameless, forlorn and forgotten, the words of the RCTS *Locomotives of the LB & SCR*, in describing that journey, have a sad ring: 'Robert Billinton would have been sorely pressed to recognize in the cavalcade of decrepit, nameless 4-4-0s that draw out of the shed roads the resplendent *Empress*, *Mafeking*, *Pretoria* and *Marlborough* he knew so well half a century earlier'. Surely he would — but of that resplendent, jaunty engine emerging from Clayton Tunnel he could certainly be proud.

Who, today, thinks of those early tunnellers as they sweep down in an HST to plunge under the Severn? This, the longest main-line tunnel in Britain, took thirteen years of blood, sweat, tears and toil to build. The challenge was daunting; for 4¼ miles, under the swirling waters of Britain's longest river, this visible manifestation of Victorian determination proclaimed itself the victor of difficulties that would have defeated lesser men. Roaring down the 1 in 100 descent from the English side or the 1 in 90 from the Welsh to the double-track, brick-lined tunnel is an experience that only dullards with no sense of history or awareness of man's mastery of the elements would ignore. Through inundation by the Great Spring, flooding by abnormal tidal wave and the great snowstorm of 18 January 1881, the work continued. Construction had commenced on 18 March 1873, but the tribulations, only some of which I have mentioned, ensured that the two headings were not joined until 16 September 1881. The first train journey through the tunnel was completed on 5 September 1885, with Daniel Gooch aboard. Regular passenger services began using the tunnel on

Right *'Tunnel Vision' indeed: the west portal of Box is visible through Middle Hill Tunnel, approached by a down HST on 14 April 1987. The A4 road overbridge obscures the outline of Box Tunnel mouth.*

The 500mm lens used to take this photograph distorts distance. The roof of the HST is just below the level of the parapet of the A4 road bridge, beyond which the dentils of Box Tunnel, half a mile away, can be identified by comparison with the picture on page 62. (See also the map on page 76.) The distortion of the track by the long lens is inaccurately alarming.

The Great Western Railway ran from Bristol to London. The Bristol-end portals of the tunnels were splendid, none more so than Brunel's classic façade of Box Tunnel, seen here on 14 April 1987. Note the milepost beside the up line.

The stately western mouth, elegance personified, conceals the bell-shaped reality, as the interior reduces to the size illustrated in the photograph of the east end of the tunnel — the cheap, or London, end.

Brunel did not include wall-recesses in which one could shelter from a passing train if working in or inspecting the interior. To be inside when an HST enters is to know fear...

1 December 1886, and the centenary of this magnificent feat of engineering has recently been celebrated. The water is still there, and so are the pumps; normal requirements see the disposal of anything between 15 and 25 million gallons of water daily.

The Severn Tunnel, unlike many of Britain's tunnels, has a well-documented history and British Rail Western Region published an official history — *The Severn Tunnel* — to mark the centenary. I recently traversed, in the cab of a diesel locomotive, what a contemporary traveller in 1886 quoted in the book described as 'the gigantic tube linking the shores of Monmouthshire and Gloucestershire' on his 'submarine journey'. It was a tremendous thrill; one was left only to imagine a similar experience on the footplate of an 'Aberdare' dragging a heavy coal-train from South Wales through this monumental undertaking.

Tunnels like the Severn earned fame, as did Brunel's Box, of which much has been written and of which numerous photographs have been taken. The tale that Brunel ensured that a pinprick of light appears through the tunnel, only in bright sunlight soon after sunrise, on one day a year — 9 April, his birthday — is amongst the more romantic fables of Britain's railway history. For the photographers, too, the emergence of a steam-hauled train from a tunnel mouth added elegance and drama to the excitement and action inherent in steam photography. To write these words brings to mind the name of artists like Ivo Peters. His portraits at Devonshire, Coombe Down, or especially at Chilcompton Tunnel, have made famous a small, short and rather insignificant bore, whilst his skill with the camera enabled him to create an attractive panorama even from a diesel-hauled train emerging from Buckhorn Weston Tunnel. The little village of Buckhorn Weston has, for railway enthusiasts, been immortalized by its tunnel, as has Kilsby and the aforementioned Box.

Railway tunnels can thus claim to have immortalized a small number of hamlets and villages that otherwise would slumber forever in obscurity. Yet many tunnels have escaped fame, and many, too, have been obliterated from the landscape — closed lines, bores boarded or bricked up with their steamy secrets, or even filled in and totally forgotten. One such is the erstwhile Clifton Hall Tunnel, of which brief mention is made in 'Last stronghold of steam' (page 157). Filled

The London end of Box Tunnel is gloomy, mysterious and rarely photographed. Approached at track level in a deep, dank cutting, it can be reached from above by the steep steps seen here. On the right is the closed and bolted tunnel entrance to the former ammunition dump, still protected by Ministry of Defence police against casual visitors. . . Brunel's original bell-arch was bricked in long ago.

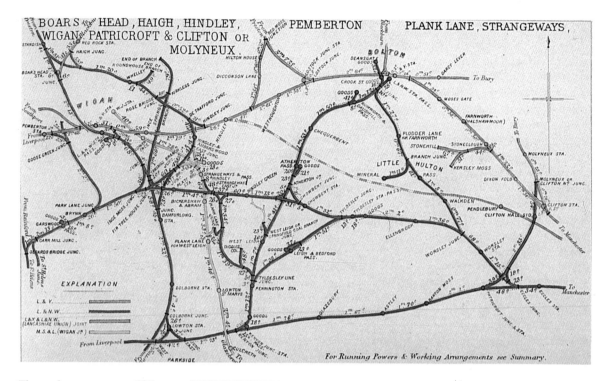

The northern entrance to Clifton Hall Tunnel, featured in this chapter, was located approximately at Clifton Hall sidings, on the far right of this 1888 map. In those days alternative routes abounded, but the separate railway companies naturally preferred to use their own lines, and there was little love lost between the L & NW and the L & Y, who could find ways to avoid the Clifton Hall line without difficulty as can be seen from a study of this map.

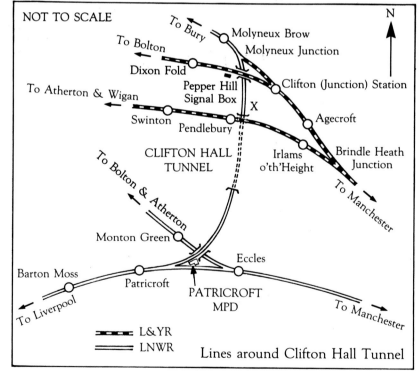

in systematically, its ends are totally invisible; it is as though it had never been. 'But some there be, who have no memorial. Their bodies are buried in peace.'

Who knows of, who remembers, Clifton Hall Tunnel? If scrubbing around in the undergrowth revealed little of the remains, what is there in mind, memory and print? My determination to dig up something developed into a minor obsession; the tale that follows encapsulates the weird fascination of and enthusiasm for knowledge of the history of our railways. Their impact on the landscape is as much an ingredient of railway interest as is information on wheel arrangements, cylinders and tractive effort of the steam locomotive. Thus my nagging inquisitiveness manifested itself in a visit to Manchester on 25 November 1986: the object was a 'return to Patricroft', as will be described in 'Last stronghold of steam', and a search for Clifton Hall Tunnel. Having completed my task in Patricroft, my companion John Brownlow, Area Operations Manager, BR (London Midland), and I set off on our search.

Have you ever set out to find a tunnel that was systematically sealed and filled, on a line that no longer exists, in the midst of a major city? Being a born hoarder, I was armed with the precise maps that I had used some twenty-four years earlier; although even then the line had been closed for more than ten years, it was nevertheless still shown

Facing south directly into the north portal of Clifton Hall Tunnel from the point 'X' on the map opposite — or into the place where the portal once stood. By 2 December 1986, when I took this photograph, few people remembered what once was here, and few if any would seem to care. Indeed, it was not easy to find the precise location. Surely anyone interested in local history, railway history or industrial archaeology would be touched by the poignancy of such a view — there is, after all, more to railways than just locomotives.

on the Ordnance Survey and Geographer's A-Z Atlas maps of the day. It was not too difficult to find where its southern end *had* been, but precisely to identify the tunnel mouth, let alone to find any trace whatsoever, was quite another matter. As we wound our way from Patricroft Station, a semi-derelict monument in its graffiti-ridden decay and disrespect to public property, my mind returned to those carefree days in Manchester in the 'sixties. We found the site of Monton Green Station on the closed and lifted Patricroft to Tyldesley line, continued up Rocky Lane and Folly Lane and turned right along the East Lancashire Road. As I followed our route on my old map, pages brown and fading at the edges, we passed the place where the East Lancs road crossed the old line. Absolutely nothing was visible. We turned left into Barton Road, and as we approached its junction with Manchester Road I swear that the back of my neck tingled.

On my map was an ink blob. It marked the location of the dingy building where my Parliamentary career nearly started, and even more nearly ended: the building that once housed, and for I know may still so do, the headquarters of the Salford West Conservative Association. There it was, one evening in 1965, that one of the most bizarre episodes of my life was enacted. Time has erased the anger but not the memory of perhaps the longest, most fruitless, frustrating and expensive journey I have ever made in search of a political career. Right at the start of my first attempt to seek adoption as a Parliamentary candidate, I found myself, following an initial interview, short-listed for Salford West. On receipt of assurances from the Agent that their selection committee had been 'most impressed' with my initial appearance before them, I agreed to appear on their final selection night, in spite of the fact that it meant a journey from Stockholm to Heathrow, the hiring of a car and a drive against the clock to Manchester in the midst of a business tour in Scandinavia — all unknown to my employer. When, on arrival at that office in Salford, the Agent greeted me with the words 'Oh Mr Adley, we tried to contact you. As the next election will probably come soon, the selection committee have decided to ask Mr Clark to stand again', my feelings may be imagined and it was the memory thereof that affected the hairs on my neck as John Brownlow and I turned into Manchester Road, those twenty-one years later.

Our car journey ended at a small new group of houses off the Bolton Road. Reference to my 1963 Manchester A to Z (6/-) was not the best guide, as the stunted parallel *culs-de-sac* had been erased by the new development. Ethel Avenue was no more. However, a narrow path bounded by a high wire fence on the site of Cliveley Road beckoned us. It crossed the Manchester Victoria–Atherton–Wigan railway line — still open — by the side of Pendlebury Station, and sloped down towards an opencast mining site. With Agecroft Power Station dominating the skyline to the north-east and the slag-ridden site of Pendlebury Colliery on our immediate left hand, we were certain that

we were in the correct area. The power station and adjacent colliery in front of us filled the plain of the River Irwell; in the distance was Pepper Hill, from the steps of which signal box I had once photographed steam-hauled commuter trains in procession from Victoria to Bolton, Preston and Blackpool some twenty-odd years before. We were in the right place; could we find any physical evidence that a railway line once ran here, and that a tunnel had emerged from the hillside above the Bolton Road?

The search for a railway-archaeological site starts with an examination of the ground for certain tell-tale remains. The most obvious is the chipped granite of a former track-bed, or, even more conclusive, the finding of old sleepers. In a very short time we found what we sought — without doubt we were on the track-bed of the Patricroft-Clifton line. As we turned to face south again, the hillside in front of us beckoned. Keeping the high wire fence on our right, we gained the foot of the hill. It was hard to imagine the gaping tunnel entrance — were we in the right place?

To compare our feelings with those of Howard Carter and his army of followers searching for the tomb of Tutankhamun would be to invite scorn and ridicule. There was no intrinsic value to what would emerge from the successful conclusion of this search; merely the inquisitiveness of a railway enthusiast seeking not buried treasure but a buried tunnel.

Looking north towards Clifton Junction: standing atop Clifton Hall Tunnel mouth (see the picture on page 65) would have provided an excellent photographic location in steam days before the tunnel's collapse closed the line in 1953.

The valley of the River Irwell somehow manages to retain a vein of greenery within an endless landscape of houses, factories, power-stations, collieries, motorways and all the other appurtenances of man's activity.

Once this was the coping stone atop the tunnel entrance, one of the few visible physical remains of this infamous but now-forgotten bore, and only discovered after lengthy search. It was a weird feeling, and richly rewarding: not maybe equivalent to the emotions of Lord Carnarvon or Howard Carter on finding Tutankhamun's tomb, but — chacun à son goût...

Nobody will ever build a tourist resort at the site of the northern portal of Clifton Hall Tunnel; this place will never feature in the glossy brochures of the package tour operators. As John Brownlow and I found the remains of the railway fencing, at what was once the cutting leading into the tunnel, we drew together, the modern railwayman and the railway romantic. It was with consummate satisfaction that we found, buried in the grass, slabs of stone that had once clearly been atop the tunnel entrance. I had found what I had come here to find.

On our way back into the city centre, we discussed the morning's adventure. John thanked me; he confessed that I had opened the door to an area of railway history which he had not previously contemplated. We visited Windsor Bridge; at the junction, work was in progress on the new link line that will fulfil the dream of those who, for more than a hundred years, have sought to link the railway systems immediately to the north and south of the city centre — the Windsor Link. As I photographed Windsor Bridge signal box, I planned to return, perhaps on a brighter day, before the publisher's deadline for this book.

Returning to London on the midday Manchester Pullman, enjoying the luxury and comfort of an excellent lunch, my determination increased further to research for information on the tragic events surrounding the demise of Clifton Hall Tunnel and the line of which it had formed part. A note to Lewis Carter-Jones, then MP for Eccles, set me on the right track. He contacted one of his constituency stalwarts, Councillor Fred Brockbank, who said he would make some enquiries for me. I wrote to *The Manchester Evening News*, seeking a response from anyone with personal memories of the tunnel's collapse. As ever, Westminster itself proved an invaluable source of information, the House of Commons Library unearthing a document published by

HMSO in 1954 for the Ministry of Transport and Civil Aviation, entitled, under the heading of Railway Accidents, a 'Report on the collapse of Clifton Hall Tunnel which occurred on 28th April 1953 at Swinton near Manchester in London Midland Region British Railways'. It is priced at 1/9d net.

Fred Brockbank went to immense trouble to prepare for me a dossier of press cuttings about the Black Harry tragedy, for thus was Clifton Hall Tunnel locally known. The headlines outline the predictable amalgam of allegation, accusation, speculation and anticipation that students of local journalism will immediately recognize. 'Tenants Intend to Fight'; 'Ald. Kerby Replies to "Accusations of Indifference"'; 'MP Asked to Speed Up Compensation'; 'Children At Play in Danger'; 'Will Disaster Rail Tunnel Become Refuse Dump?'.

That the tunnel was known as Black Harry has added a touch of mystery and intrigue to the tale. Tunnels have very different characteristics from viaducts and bridges; and a different public image, too. My letter to *The Manchester Evening News* brought me five letters from people, all of which provided me with interesting, personal information. Mr C. E. Bowker of Swinton recalls 'very happy memories of this line, as my previous address, at Monton, Eccles, gave the view of the embankment that carried the line, just a short distance from the house'. He tells me that the name Black Harry Tunnel was 'inspired by the black whiskered foreman in charge of the workers at the time the line was built'.

From Mr B. Edmondson of Salford came a detailed description of the line, delightfully illustrated by his nine-year-old daughter Claire. He says that most of the trains that used the line were hauled by Fowler '7F' 0-8-0s. How I should love to have found a photograph of these big-boilered machines on the line, 175 of which were built between 1929 and 1932.

The plan contained in the Parliamentary report referred to in the text.

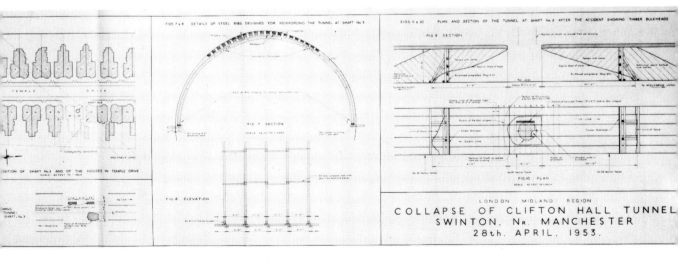

Mr J. G. Smith of Swinton lived with his family in a house above the line. With his school friends he would walk through the tunnel after Sunday School. He recalls that Clifton Hall colliery, on the line, was closed 'early this century after a terrible explosion. Most of the casualties, 175 men and boys, are buried in my local churchyard'.

From Mr R. Davies, whose father and grandfather were both engine drivers, came some professional information culled from his experience as a Train Recorder in Patricroft Station signal box, as well as relief at Ordsall Lane Station and Eccles boxes, the latter still very much in use. He recalls 'the movement of chlorine tanks up the branch line to the tunnel for safety in case of air-raid. Usually about 3 or 4 tanks would be brought along and, depending on the weather, they would be taken beyond the Patricroft Station's platform towards Winton. On a signal from the "box" the driver would try to pick up as much speed as possible to "belt" the tanks up the embankment and the curve. Many is the time that they had to go back and try again, especially if the line was wet, as they had to make sure that they didn't jump the line on the curve. Sometimes it took two engines to do the job. There was usually a good shower of sparks from the wheels/rails and the smoke stack.'

The last of my most helpful correspondents wrote on 19 January 1987 from Swinton. Confirming the transportation of chlorine tanks through the tunnel, Mr J. Platt tells me of his childhood in Worsley Road, when his mother would say 'there goes the 8.45 through the tunnel'. 'Little did I think that one day I would be working under the tunnel'. He recalls that, during the Second World War, tanks of liquid chlorine gas were stored inside Black Harry. He writes 'There were many leakages under the tunnel and we had to wear a service respirator when attending to these leaks and in my and my mate's opinion these were the cause of the collapse of the tunnel. One of my workmates, William Breckles, who lived at Bolton was presented at Buckingham Palace with the BEM medal — for turning off a valve during one of these leaks. Unfortunately he did not live long afterwards as it affected his lungs.'

Reading the report on the collapse of the tunnel reveals no mention of chlorine gas leakages as a possible cause of destabilization; my chemical knowledge is non-existent, but enquiries of the better-educated, such as Emma, daughter of my secretary Kay Dixon, seem to cast doubt on the likelihood of chlorine attacking bricks and mortar whilst recording the possibility that any metal supports in the tunnel could have been affected. As we know that the tunnel was built on a line opened in 1850 and that its early records were lost, we may never find the answer to this conundrum.

My search for any physical remains of Clifton Hall Tunnel has awakened in me a nascent interest in what, to some, may seem a morbid subject. Surely not, though, to true railway enthusiasts? Frankly I enjoyed searching for the remains of Clifton Hall under the shadow of Agecroft Colliery as much as wandering around Aspendos, not least because nobody else was there... solitude enables one's imagination to explore the unknown. As I write these words, my interest has been awakened in Devizes Tunnel, which seems sadly to have escaped the attention of most of the photographers of note. The Devizes line suffered the inevitable fate of many cross-country branches. Services were reduced, connections lengthened. By 1962, on 'busy' Saturdays there was but one eastbound train from Devizes; it terminated at Savernake. London-bound travellers were 'offered' a 'connection' with an hour's wait here in the shape of a train to Newbury, where a further change was entailed. Arrival at Paddington for our intrepid rail traveller was some four hours after departure from this important Wiltshire town. Final closure of the line, the history of which is delightfully recorded by Nigel Bray in *A Wiltshire Railway Remembered — The Devizes Branch*, followed the running of the last train on 16 April 1966. The 190-yard tunnel ran beneath Devizes Castle, its foundations being 'twenty or thirty feet below the level of the old moat'.

Little could anyone have anticipated the notoriety that Devizes Tunnel was to earn in the summer of 1987. It leapt to the headlines as the shooting club of Michael Ryan, the Hungerford mass murderer. This paragraph, always intended for this book, awaited completion pending a long-awaited visit to the Brunel bore. By the time, accompanied by my intrepid secretary/accomplice Kay Dixon, we paid our visit to Devizes Tunnel, we knew that routine railway interest would be subsumed — not by us, but by the tunnel's tenants, the Wiltshire Shooting Centre — under a blanket of concern about MP's attitudes to the gun laws. But let me firmly resist any temptation to stray from Brunel's route.

Built for broad guage double track, the stonework inside the tunnel remains intact, and in excellent condition. Whether the cordite emission from today's activity has a greater or lesser effect on the fabric of the tunnel, is hard to say.

Happily my Parliamentary colleagues, aware of my idiosyncrasies, are always willing to help me, through local contacts, to explore the remains of old railways in their constituencies. British Rail, too, are generous with the time of regional personnel who doubtless have better things to do than to humour me. However, I console myself and justify my nuisance-factor by acting as their unpaid self-appointed supporter in Parliament. As they have recently appointed, for the first time, a Tourism Officer, I look forward to discussing the creation of railway-historical tours of closed as well as of still-open lines. Fanciful it may be, but unlikely places have become tourist attractions, and railway tunnels seem to me to be a source of untapped special-interest material.

Where shall we terminate this ramble of tunnels disused and still in service? Where else am I covering my tracks? Clifton Hall collapsed

Haslingden Tunnel, soon after the track was lifted, on 4 June 1968. Northwards from Bury, at Stubbins Junction, the line to Rawtenstall bore away north-eastwards, whilst the Accrington line ran through Helmshore, Haslingden and over the fearsome Baxenden Bank (see also the picture on page 160). The East Lancashire Railway is undertaking a splendid project hereabouts. The exposure necessary to illustrate the wet tunnel walls inevitably causes violent contrast with the bright light outside.

and was closed. Devizes, with its castle, decays and dims with the memory of its line. What has happened to the long tunnel under Bolsover Castle, the deterioration of which itself led to the closure of the erstwhile Lancashire, Derbyshire & East Coast Railway line to Chesterfield. Shall I ask Dennis Skinner or Tony Benn? Who now remembers the weekdays-only service between Chesterfield, Langwith Junction, Dukeries Junction and Lincoln? Who, in Bolsover today, recalls the last train through the tunnel of a Saturday night — the 10.15 from Chesterfield to Mansfield, calling at Arkwright Town, Bolsover, Scarcliffe, Langwith Junction, Warsop and Mansfield (Great Central)? Trains to Bolsover?

Covering those tracks under Bolsover Castle is a pleasure so far denied to me. One day time may permit me to make a pilgrimage there. A journey by road from Chesterfield, past Bolsover Castle, in August 1987 provided no time at all for railway exploration, but sufficient opportunity to glimpse the potential interest of an area rich in contrasts, from the castle itself in its dominant position, through to the ghost of the Great Central hereabouts. There is much to explore. Who thought of photographing tunnel mouths on lines closing in the 1960s? As an end in itself, all too few. It was ignorance, rather than recording for posterity, that found me at Haslingden Tunnel on 4 June 1968.

Not until I got there, camera hopefully in hand, did I realize that railway archaeology rather than railway operation was to be my reward. Perhaps the photograph I took, from the tunnel mouth, may give a flavour of the opportunities lost and gone forever.

Of Staple Hill Tunnel, in the suburbs of Bristol and within my erstwhile constituency of Bristol North-East, have I made passing mention in 'Last stronghold of steam'. It now forms part of the walk and cycle-track based on the erstwhile Midland Railway route between Bath and Bristol, or, to be more accurate, of the line from Bath to Mangotsfield Junction where it then joined the main Bristol to Gloucester line of the Midland Railway. Here is a track one can walk, and the eastern portal of Staple Hill Tunnel is the place, perforce, to stop and ponder...

Tales about tunnels are legion. One of the strangest concerned the Portway Tunnel at the foot of Bristol's Avon gorge. During the blitz on the city in 1941, the tunnel became initially a shelter, then a haven, and finally a hostel; firstly for tens, then for hundreds and ultimately for upwards of three thousand people. The disused tunnel, however, was itself thoroughly unsafe, part having been condemned as dangerous. Yet in time of danger from enemy air-raids, the tunnel provided what seemed a safe refuge, although had a bomb landed directly on top, the carnage would have wreaked a tragedy of which even the Luftwaffe would not have been deliberately capable. Each evening before the

As prospective Conservative Parliamentary Candidate for Bristol North-East, I tried to save the former Midland line through my constituency from closure. Staple Hill Tunnel, the west end of which I photographed from the station, is seen here in August 1969, just before the line was closed, although Staple Hill and the other Bristol suburban stations had already done so. Prior to 'rationalization' and complete closure, trains from the West Country to Birmingham and the north, as well as Bristol-Gloucester services via this, the former Midland Railway route, lingered on for a few more months. My ideas for retaining, reinvigorating and even developing a suburban railway system in the area were derided; now they have been purloined by others, claimed as their own, and are better received as road traffic slowly clogs Bristol to a standstill.

Darkness and mystery accentuated by the curvature of the line, the eastern mouth of Tytherington tunnel on the erstwhile Thornbury branch of the Midland Railway. Photographed on 28 July 1986, the 7½ mile line from Yate to Thornbury opened on 2 September 1872, closed to passengers in 1944 and completely in 1966. The track was lifted. Surprisingly, as can be seen, the line was reopened from Yate to Tytherington Quarry, situated just beyond the tunnel: a rare re-opening indeed.

bombers came, families trekked often for miles, with bedding, utensils and food, in prams and on bicycles, to take their places underground until dawn and the 'all clear' came.

As the weeks went by, Portway Tunnel became a cross between an air raid shelter, a church mission hall and a soup kitchen. As the year wore on it became occupied by day as well as by night, its 'inhabitants' joining in wartime camaraderie that knew no fear of overcrowding, nor distaste of insanitary conditions. Sunday religious services were held, nursery school activities were organized, pets were 'adopted', even Christmas in 1941 was celebrated in the tunnel.

Famous tunnels; closed and disused tunnels; in-filled tunnels; forgotten tunnels; what is there left? Somewhere, a simple tunnel, unremarkable, still in use, perhaps on a freight-only line, survives against the odds today. Indeed it does — at Tytherington, once in Gloucestershire on an obscure line to a hidden quarry, is the tunnel of that name — still dripping, still eerie, and still open. The Midland Railway's ertswhile Thornbury branch, from its junction with the main Bristol-Gloucester line at Yate, closed to passengers in 1944 and completely in 1966. I visited the line in July 1964 and photographed my young nephews Nicholas and Timothy Pople for posterity. When the line closed completely it seemed unthinkable that trains could ever again traverse it.

On 28 July 1986 I returned to Tytherington Tunnel, now just short of the terminus of the line. Of narrow bore, it is approached from the Yate end on a bend and in a cutting. Intrigue and expectation, aligned to a dripping wet 'summer' day, create their own atmosphere and aroma in any tunnel. In a moment one leaves behind the daylight and, before one's eyes become accustomed to the dark, the fear of the unknown, unseen world of the tunnel encompasses you. If the line is still open to traffic, the thought is never far distant that one's ears, in that silent world below the earth, may fail you... If, like Tytherington, the tunnel is curved, no light is visible to guide and to comfort. Dampness seems often to be a feature of our journey into darkness. Maybe ghosts of bygone steam locomotives lurk here...

Tytherington tunnel, a mere 224 yards long, is known to few. Its curvature invests it with deep darkness, a darkness not of romance or excitement, but of that ethereal gloominess and mystery that is the stuff of tunnels. My two visits were separated by 22 years, but I never traversed it by rail.

Not many miles away, in the adjacent county of Wiltshire, is perhaps the most famous, arguably the most elegant and certainly the most legendary railway tunnel in Britain. Work commenced with trial shafts on Box Tunnel in 1836. At the zenith of construction, 4,000 navvies and 300 horses sweated and strained, and their community saw the

Exactly twenty-two years earlier — the same tunnel mouth, from the inside looking out. Silhouetted are my nephews Nicholas and Timothy Pople, the latter studying the Ordnance Survey map. Jackie Jenkins joined us in our exploration that day in July 1964, some two years before the line's total closure, as mentioned on the left.

The extremes of darkness and light make these amongst the most difficult photographs to take successfully, as is self-evident.

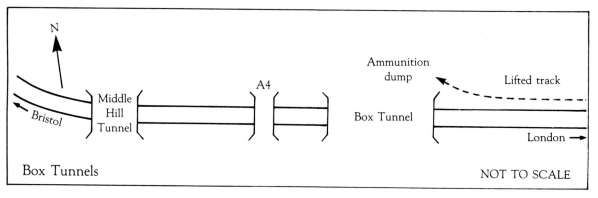

Box Tunnels   NOT TO SCALE

behavioural excesses associated with tunnel-building gangs. They drank, they fought, they terrorized the village communities; and a hundred died before the great hole was completed. Yet completed it was — Brunel would not be beaten by a mere hillside — and it was the writing of this chapter that finally compelled me to go on foot to imbibe the atmosphere of a place to and through which I have travelled times too numerous to count.

Before I recount that memorable afternoon, Wednesday 15 April 1987, let me utter a solemn warning: do *not* attempt a rail-side visit to Box without permission, without accompaniment by a BR official, without an orange vest, and without a proper awareness of and respect for the consummate danger of the place in the era of the High Speed Train. To be in that tunnel simultaneously with an HST is truly an awesome experience, and he who is not suitably afeared is a fool. I was therefore grateful both for the presence and the personality of BR Bristol Area Signalling Inspector Jim Barnes, my guide and mentor some months earlier when we visited Tytherington, Yate, Westerleigh and Mangotsfield in seeking the remains of the Midland Railway in the Bristol area.

Jim Barnes joined the GWR in 1942 as a telegraphist at Stapleton Road, Bristol. Together, as we were at Box on 15 April, we inevitably talked of Brunel, six days after his birthday. That 9 April was the great man's birthday may not have occurred to the writer of the first recorded report of the now-legendary phenomenon of the sun shining directly through the tunnel at sunrise on this day in 1842, the year after the full opening of the tunnel. Argument still rages on this romantic legend, yet nobody doubts that it occurs, and Jim Barnes took a splendid photograph to prove it. The sun would not go round the bend of Tytherington's 224 yards, but it undoubtedly does penetrate the 3,123 yards of Box at sunrise on Brunel's birthday...

The Great Western Railway runs from Bristol to London, not from London to Bristol. The imperious west portal of Box Tunnel at the Bristol end, contrasts dramatically with the plain, austere eastern entrance to the great bore. Indeed, Box itself attracts such attention that the nearby Middle Hill tunnel, approximately half a mile west of Box, is rarely mentioned, yet its impressive portals would certainly not pass unremarked on railways other than the Great Western, even though it is but 198 yards long. Jim Barnes quite rightly refused to allow me to walk through, lest an HST catch us unawares. Approached by a bend from the westerly direction, the view looking east through Middle Hill gives a splendid telescoped perspective view of Box, albeit impaired and visually distorted by the A4 road bridge that crosses the line a few yards to the east of Box Tunnel itself.

Despite the unimpressive eastern portal of Box Tunnel, it is nevertheless worthy of further brief mention. Approached through a steep-sided brick-lined cutting, it is gloomy and remote. Added mystery surrounds the now bricked-up entrance, a few yards to the east of Box's eastern portal, and on the north side of the line, to what was reputed to be, during the Second World War, the largest ammunition dump in Britain. Miles of underground tunnel created from the Bath stone excavations were developed into a place I have yet to explore. How 'closed' they are may be deduced from the fact that a Ministry of Defence policeman was alongside us within minutes of our — quite legal — arrival on the scene, via a flight of steep stone steps down to track level from the wooded landscape above the eastern portal of Box Tunnel. There is much for me yet to discover.

If tunnels still in use are eyries where the clammy hand of darkness touches the back of the neck, then closed and disused bores are certainly not places for the faint-hearted. Who now has taken possession of this dark and silent world? Are there villains lurking there, seeking a safe hideaway? Or madmen perhaps, or fiends so foul or disfigured that they dare not face the light? Or rats, grown huge and yet hungry? Or ghosts, not of the steam engines that helped to line the tunnel sides with soot, but haunted souls who died when hacking this cavern through the rock. Can I escape? Should I go on, in hope that the far end is not sealed permanently? Should I turn back — or has someone suddenly boarded-in the hole through which, minutes before, I squeezed to satisfy my curiosity and prove my manliness. This is the railway; here still is the spirit of adventure, the challenge that Brunel and Stephenson overcame. Lesser men than they would have been daunted, but they dared. March on, march on, march on . . .

SOMERSET OR DORSET?

Selecting chapter titles is an important ingredient in the composition of my books. My thanks for this one are therefore due to Kenneth Abel, Chief Executive of Dorset County Council. In a letter to me dated 24 July 1986 he enclosed a copy of his letter to the Local Government Boundary Commission for England, in which he submits a report from the Policy and Resources Committee of the County Council regarding the review of county boundaries by non-metropolitan counties pursuant to the Local Government Act of 1972. My copy together with those sent to my Parliamentary colleagues Nicholas Baker and Jim Spicer were sent as a courtesy to Dorset's three MPs whose constituencies have common boundaries with either Devon, Somerset, Wiltshire or Hampshire. In my case, minor changes are proposed to the Dorset-Hampshire border; however contentious these may be to the handful of people — and the larger number of cattle and trees — involved, it is reasonably certain that they are of no interest whatsoever to readers of this book. So, you are asking, 'what is this all about?'. Let me now explain.

Having perused the proposals in my constituency, for Ringwood Forest, Avon Valley, Sopley Park, Chewton Bunny, and those in the Highcliffe-Somerford area revolving around the line of the railway, I flicked the pages to Appendix A, there to see a detailed recommendation from the South Somerset District Council, supported by Somerset County Council, to transfer from Dorset to Somerset the Babylon Hill/Yeovil Junction Station area. Thus was ignited the spark of inspiration, if that be the word, for the title of this chapter.

There seems no good planning reason to transfer Yeovil Junction from Dorset to Somerset, any more than there is to transfer London Airport from Hillingdon to Westminster, or Hurn Airport from Christchurch to Bournemouth. Just because the name is artificially attached to an adjacent big town is no reason whatsoever to spite history at the behest of urban sprawl. Indeed, the land between Yeovil Junction Station and Yeovil Pen Mill, let alone the erstwhile Town Station, is an outstandingly clear example of how one county, Dorset, has controlled and prevented urban sprawl; would that Dorset's planners were as dedicated to this proposition at the eastern end of

Far left *In August 1986, the distinctive lattice post, finial, home and distant upper quadrant semaphore arms and appropriate sign still protect the single line linking Southern and Western regions at this key inter-regional junction. However, both the formerly double-track parallel lines have long since been singled. Note the angle to the line at which this signal is placed.*

Top left *Gradient posts of both Southern and Great Western railways decorate the track hereabouts. This one, on the Southern line, stands about one-third of a mile north from Yeovil Junction box: 1 in 230 up to the Junction, 1 in 1900 up towards Pen Mill and Western territory. Quite a collector's item, methinks...*

Bottom left *As with signals and gradient posts, Great Western and Southern cast-iron mileposts distinguish and still adorn the parallel tracks 'twixt Pen Mill and Junction stations, providing interest for railway historians. Here, marking the commencement of Southern territory, is theirs, still in situ in 1987.*

Extracted from the 1888 Railway Clearing House map book is this magnification of the Yeovil area. Green lines are LSWR, yellow are GWR. Today, a century later, the main change is the closure of the GW line westwards from Pen Mill — incidentally spelt incorrectly here, but corrected in later editions. The station shown as 'GW & L & SW joint' is Town; it, of course, no longer exists. About half a mile south of Pen Mill the two lines — now both single track — make a junction, providing an essential link between Western and Southern territory (see the map opposite). The line to Clifton Maybank, and all the railway there, has long since disappeared, but the name may yet appear in future rationalization hereabouts (see page 93).

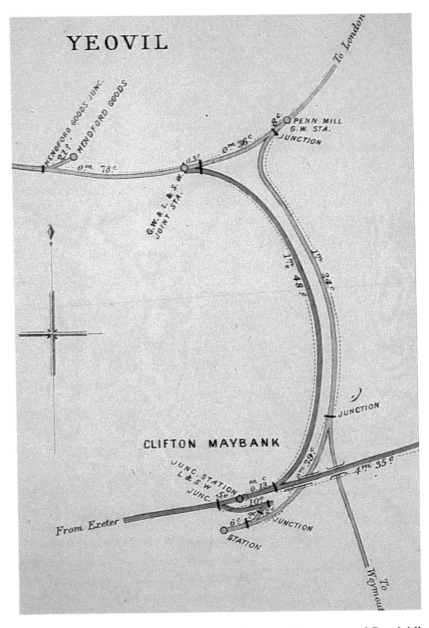

the county. That stretch of countryside 'twixt Junction and Pen Mill through which and on which the railway runs is a small but quite charmed piece of unspoiled England. Man's only intrusion is the railway itself. To walk the track, from the SR semaphore signal gantry at the Junction, northwards to the bridge where the A30 road crosses the railway at the neck of the line at the entry to Pen Mill Station, is to enjoy solace, to ponder the fate of the lifted track on two sides of the triangle to Town Station, and to appreciate the presence of the

ever-dwindling number of semaphore signals still in use. Yet it is much
more, for Yeovil was — and indeed visibly still is — the point of contact
between the two great railway companies, GWR and LSWR (and
subsequently SR), that fought for dominance hereabouts one hundred
and forty years ago. Signals, mileposts, chairs, bridge-plates; for the
observant railway historian the interest remains infinite.

For me, Yeovil represents the embodiment of my frustration; an
anguished example of missed opportunities, of failure to create or to
capitalize on opportunities for railway photography at the end of the
steam era. On 21 August 1963, for reasons that my struggling memory

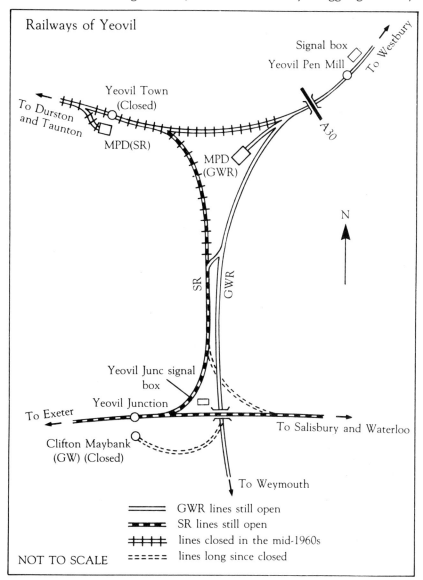

Railways of Yeovil

Signal box
Yeovil Pen Mill

To Westbury

To Durston
and Taunton

Yeovil Town
(Closed)

A30

MPD(SR)

MPD
(GWR)

N

SR

GWR

Yeovil Junc signal
box

Yeovil Junction

To Exeter

To Salisbury and Waterloo

Clifton Maybank
(GW) (Closed)

To Weymouth

———— GWR lines still open
━▮━▮ SR lines still open
╫╫╫╫ lines closed in the mid-1960s
NOT TO SCALE ══════ lines long since closed

By comparison with the map on
the opposite page, this diagram
attempts to portray the current
Yeovil scene but with pre-
nationalization nomenclature. As
may be seen, the link 'twixt the
erstwhile SR and GWR lines
now marks the approximate
regional boundary.

The motive power depots have
both long since been demolished.
At the time of writing, GWR
and SR semaphore signals,
gradient posts and mileposts still
adorn the trackside (see page 78).

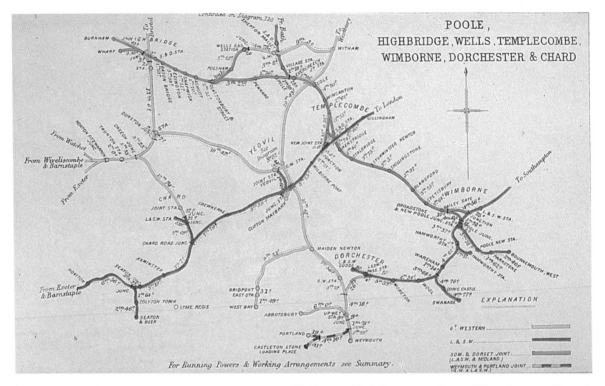

Not much more than an excuse to include another of the splendid Railway Clearing House maps, again dated 1888. 'Yeovil' does not feature in the heading, but the town sits, centre stage, on this map. Whilst today's equivalent map shows a decimated railway system, the one line not yet built in 1888 is the GW main line westwards, from Castle Cary to a point west of Langport, where it joined the Yeovil branch of the former Bristol & Exeter Railway at Curry Rivel Junction, itself about 6½ miles from Durston Junction shown here. Perhaps the miracle is the very survival of the Westbury-Yeovil-Weymouth line.

cannot now recall, I travelled by train from Waterloo to Yeovil. Naturally my camera accompanied me. My first photograph, at Waterloo, was of Bulleid 'Merchant Navy' 'Pacific' No 35020 *Bibby Line* awaiting the road from the terminus to back down to Nine Elms, having worked in on an up morning express to London. My final shot that memorable day was also at Waterloo on my return that evening (see page 22-3). My catalogue notes state '5 engines visible at Waterloo: seven platform view'. I recorded the numbers of three: Urie 'S15' 4-6-0 No 30499 and two BR Standard '3' 2-6-2Ts Nos 82018/9. No 30499 is one of the charmed handful of Britain's steam stock that survived the cutter's torch by virtue of acquisition by Dai Woodham for scrapping at his Barry yard. Once this fact presented itself to me in writing this chapter, it spurred me to undertake and complete a task neglected for years, namely to catalogue my Barry photographs and thereafter to scour the records of my 1962-68 photography in order to match the two. The results may appear in a future book, but for the day of my 1963 Yeovil visit no less than four engines photographed that day were subsequently seen at Barry; just another minor act of pleasurable reminiscence extracted from the task of writing. I digress.

Friday 1 August 1986, then, was the day selected for my 'return to Yeovil'. Living not far away in Dorset, the prospect of a really early start was not too daunting. Erstwhile visits entailed the acquisition of the dismal knowledge of the total obliteration of Yeovil Town Station and engine shed, now replaced by — what else? — a supermarket car-park. How well the decline and fall of steam is commemorated in our towns and cities by the contemporaneous decline of shopping where *people* served you. It is a sad but statistical fact that the emergence of self-service shopping is concomitant with the increase of shoplifting. Yeovil today has lost its town centre railway station and many of its decent individual shops, not to mention its railway connection with the county town of Taunton. However, it still has much to offer the returning visitor, as has already been mentioned, in its visible links with inter-railway rivalry and history, in that rare, unspoiled and largely unvisited stretch of country between its two remaining stations, Junction (in Dorset) and Pen Mill (in Somerset). Why not join me in a few hours' reminiscence?

As with much of my life, that day, 1 August 1986, was heavily influenced, insofar as it related to my activities, by my wife Jane. Railway enthusiasts' spouses fall into three categories: sullen, resentful and jealous of an interest that they neither share nor comprehend; total immersion — rare but not unknown; or tolerant, reasonably supportive, willing to encourage and secretly appreciating the tenets of history and geography that are an inseparable inheritance of our enthusiasm. Jane is one of the latter, able to appreciate a good railway-photographic location, able to recognise an 'A4' from a 'King', but not perhaps attuned to the attraction of the scarcity value of a Crosti-boilered '9F', if you appreciate the dividing line I seek to draw. Thus it was that, awakened as she asserted by my snoring at 05.10 on that August morning, she proclaimed lest I still be enjoying my sleep, that it looked a 'perfect day for that wonderful early light which so enhances railway photography'. Thus I was goaded into action and left home, suitably equipped with camera and fruit, before 05.30.

It *was* a magnificent morning. Mist hung over the fields giving an ethereal appearance to the Friesians surrounding us. The lightening sky was cloudless to the west as I set forth in that direction. At that hour the A30 was deserted. Like the 'Atlantic Coast Express' before me, I sped by Templecombe through Milborne Port and Sherborne, but, unlike the SR's crack express of yesteryear, I pulled into the yard at Yeovil Pen Mill Station, just after 6.0 am.

Total insanity might have seen me endeavouring to photograph Yeovil's first passenger departure of the day, 04.55 from Junction, but even on 21 June such light as might be available on midsummer day would need to be cast on a subject of some interest; alas, today's railway scene on what remains of the LSWR main line merits not that description. My 'target', therefore, was the arrival at Pen Mill of the 05.55 from Westbury, due in at its terminating point here at 06.39. The actual axis of the line at this point is north-east (towards Castle Cary) — south-west, so geography and the structure of the station dictate the selection of one's photographic vantage point.

Overleaf *Great Western, Southern and BR Standard engines were on shed at 72C Yeovil Town on 21 August 1963, amongst which was '4575' Class 2-6-2T No 5563 and Standard '4' 2-6-0 No 76005. The '4575' Class of Great Western 2-6-2Ts, introduced in 1927, was a modified version of the Churchward '45xx' Class of 1906, which itself was developed from the '44xx' Class. Designated for use on light branch work, it can be seen that the tank engine, seen here alongside the 2-6-0 from a class introduced by BR in 1953, is indeed from an earlier generation. No 5563 was withdrawn from Yeovil MPD in September 1964; No 76005, a Salisbury engine at the date of this photograph, was withdrawn from Bournemouth shed (70F) when steam finally finished on Southern Region in July 1967. The site is now a car park.*

Spot on time, the locomotive-hauled train hove into view out of the brilliant low sun. The line curves in to Yeovil sharply, threading its way around the contours of Babylon Hill. I cannot pretend to be aroused or excited by the sight of a diesel locomotive, but the working railway presents its own charm and challenge even to the most amateur and incompetent camera-practitioner. Having fumed and fiddled around with my 500mm lens on its tripod, and prayed as ever that my too-clever-by-half Canon A1 had not bamboozled and beaten me yet again, I clicked merrily away. The Class '33' brought its five coaches past me, ran alongside Pen Mill's signal box and came to a stand alongside the down platform. The station still retains its rather unusual layout. The up line is actually served by a platform on both sides, so that the down platform is an island, itself lying between the up and down lines.

At one time, Pen Mill Station had an overall roof, long since gone. The up line is now signalled for reversible working since the demise of the line (and trains) to Durston. When a down train is not crossing an up train at the station, the former often uses the up platform as it is beside the station entrance and drive, thus making life easier for passengers. Speed limits through the station remain.

Changed circumstances are reflected in the number of railwaymen employed at Pen Mill. In 1909 the Stationmaster oversaw two booking clerks, a foreman and 33 other men, including guards and brakemen. Today there are seven.

Obviously the track layout is both simplified and reduced by the closure not only of the goods shed and sidings, but by the demise of the line to Yeovil Town Station and thence to Durston and Taunton, not to mention the engine shed and coaling-stage, closed in 1959. The Yeovil-Taunton (actually Yeovil-Durston) line closed on 15 June 1964; trains in that direction started from Pen Mill up line, which was, and remains, signalled in both directions, as already mentioned, and still with GWR lower-quadrant semaphore signals. That at the south end still has its route-indicator attachment, but the diamond track-circuit indicator visible in old photographs is no longer there. At the base of this signal is the silent testimony to the singling of the former double-tracked railways running south from Pen Mill. 'Commencement of Token Section' indicates that the appearance of double-track between Pen Mill and Yeovil Junction is an illusion.

Before attempting to describe that haven of peaceful railway nostalgia that is the landscape between the two remaining Yeovil stations, let us return to Pen Mill and the 06.39 arrival of the 05.55 from Westbury. Having completed its journey, the locomotive is at the southern end of the down platform; it has then to be manoeuvred to depart from the up platform at the head of the 06.55 Yeovil to Cardiff through train. This is accomplished as follows. The locomotive is uncoupled and called forward by the lower right-hand signal on the gantry at

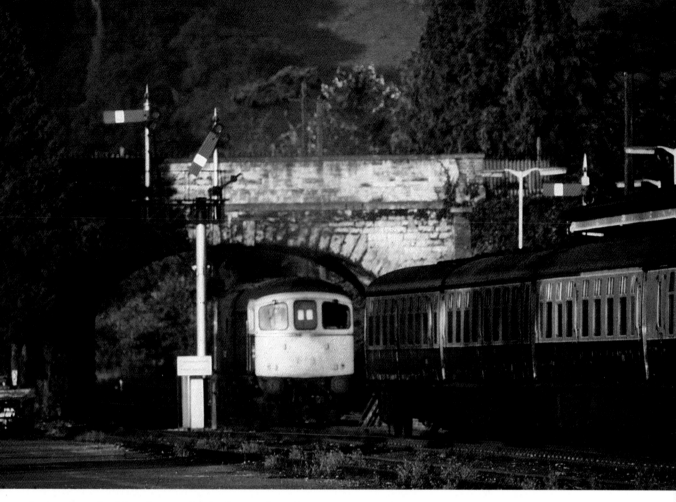

the south end of the down side platform. The Class '33' proceeds under the A30 road-bridge immediately to the south of the platform. Having cleared the points beyond the bridge — a single line only now runs under the bridge — the locomotive then sets back, light engine, through the station on the up line, past the signal box, and is brought to a stand. It then crosses back on to the down line, runs up to its coaches and is coupled up at the 'north' end. The signal at the south end of the down side which released the Class '33', light engine, a couple of minutes previously, is now pulled off again, and the locomotive propels its train out of the down side platform, on under the bridge, and, via the single line, comes to a stand beyond the points. The train with the locomotive now at its head, completes the final stage of its empty stock working by running forward into the up platform where, as already mentioned, it now forms the 06.55 train to Cardiff Central. This is quite a useful train for me in connection with the Cardiff Holiday Inn, where my pannier tank No 9629 now stands sentinel outside the hotel although, annoyingly, in the latest timetable change this train terminates at Bristol Temple Meads: my journey to Swansea by rail entails two changes, with alternative possibilities, but I digress again...

The manoeuvres involving the locomotive off the 05.55 from Westbury, forming the 06.55 Pen Mill to Cardiff train on 1 August 1986, are described in the text. Here the Class '33' has been detached from its stock, and runs forward under the A30 road overbridge at the south end of Pen Mill station. It will then run round its train, back through Pen Mill up platform. The erstwhile line to Town, and to Taunton, bore away to the right immediately under this bridge (see the map on page 81). GWR lower quadrant signals are disappearing fast from the railway scene. Note the fumes from the diesel locomotive.

Previous page *Classified '1P',
'54xx' Class 0-6-0PT No 5410
stands in Yeovil Town station on
21 August 1963. It will return to
Yeovil Junction as part of the
daily shuttle service between
Town, Junction and Pen Mill
stations. The station was closed,
the lines westward to Taunton,
east to Pen Mill and south to
Junction lifted, and the railway
obliterated in Yeovil town centre.
The site today is as dull and
depressing as it is possible to find
— a car-park serving a
supermarket.*

*The '54xx' pannier tanks were
introduced by Collett in 1931;
they were designed for light
passenger work and were push-*

All this light engine/empty stock working took place on 1 August 1986 in brilliant early morning sunshine. The bright red of those GWR lower quadrants; the stone bridge; the green hills close by; the distinctive outline of the signal box; all these help to coagulate into a familiar scene — 'The Railway'. There is, of course, one huge irreplaceable gap in this vintage scene, a gap so large as to be unbridgeable if one is correctly trying to relive the mood of yesteryear. But, faced with the choice of a non-steam railway or no railway, one must make the most of what is left to enjoy. As I write these words, Yeovil is as good a place as any — but for how long?

Having witnessed the departure for Cardiff, and not wanting to 'waste' any early morning sunlight, I set off post-haste from Pen Mill for Yeovil Junction, hoping perhaps that late running might enable me to photograph the 06.09 Salisbury to Exeter train, due away from Yeovil Junction at 07.02. At this hour there was little traffic in Yeovil. The direct road route takes one over the road bridge which crossed the line from Pen Mill at the east end of Yeovil Town Station. With

appropriate pangs for the past and revulsion for its replacement, I sped on, out of the town, across the border into Dorset. With my pass safely in my possession, I parked in the Junction Station car park and headed for the signal box.

Alan Cox was expecting me, although maybe not at this hour. Signalmen, perhaps above all others, epitomize the unique attributes that set the true railwayman apart from lesser mortals. To men like Alan Cox, and to Jim Maidment whom we shall meet shortly, being on the railway is not a job, it is a way of life. History lives in the railwayman's family, and Alan is no exception. Real life, not a railway enthusiast's novel, placed in that box that day a man who was formerly a Relief Signalman at Stalbridge, Shillingstone and Sturminster Newton (see the map on page 82). His father, still hale and hearty, had been Station Master at Stalbridge. Somehow the glamour of the Somerset & Dorset Joint Railway attached more to its passage through the former county. Places like Templecombe, Evercreech Junction, Masbury Summit, Chilcompton Tunnel, Midford — the list seems endless — are better known to the S & D's hordes of admirers than are the three Dorset towns where Alan Cox saw duty. Yet for those of us who live in S & D country in Dorset, the pains and pangs are just as great south of the county boundary. The railway bridge at Stur; the level crossing at Stalbridge with the rails still clearly visible; the bridge over the river at Shillingstone — these are almost daily and visible reminders of our raped heritage. It was these thoughts, that sunny early morning, that flashed through my mind as Alan Cox and I became acquainted. The Great Western Railway, or at least its successor, Western Region, had seen to it that Bath to Weymouth survived, but that Bath to Bournemouth perished. The old enemy had his way. Alan Cox was a casualty of the vengeance of railway history, but at least he survived to tell the tale as a working railwayman. Others were not so young in 1967 nor so fortunate.

Having commenced this chapter, and indeed entitled it by reference to local government boundaries, the theme of that last paragraph and of local government changes merits mention of the pursuit of an idea of mine that has emerged from the combined effect of the closure of the S & D and the changes in local government boundaries that transferred parts of south-west Hampshire into Dorset. This change, which encompassed Bournemouth (which nobody really wanted) as well as a part of my constituency, was more than just a change of county. For whereas Hampshire is in 'south-east England', Dorset is in 'south-west England'. At a stroke of the legislative pen, therefore, an area that formerly looked to London as its regional 'capital' now perforce was centred on Bristol and, for some services, Exeter. Thus was created the new transport axis requirement for south-east Dorset, to the County of Avon; or, in more familiar parlance, perhaps, for the Bournemouth area to Bristol, via Bath.

pull fitted. They supplanted the 'M7' 0-4-4T engines on these services a few days before this photograph was taken, and soon after Western Region took over here from the Southern. Yeovil Town MPD, 72C in Southern days, became 83E on 9 September 1963: it is on the right, with the cab of another pannier tank just visible by the yellow board. No 5410, one of the last three survivors of this class of twenty-five engines, was withdrawn a few weeks later, stored at Swindon and finally cut up at Birds, Risca, in October 1964.

Opposite *Noxious fumes rise from the roof-vents of the Class '33' as the SR upper quadrant signal lifts. The Salisbury-Meldon via Westbury train will run past Yeovil Junction box to gain the LSWR main line westbound towards Exeter. This roundabout route is necessitated by the singling of the main line westwards from Salisbury — a decision of penny-pinching shortsightedness resulting from age-old railway rivalry.*

To pinpoint the location of this photograph, taken in August 1986, see the map on page 82. The filled hoppers on the left of this picture will shortly be taken to Taunton — but not by the now-lifted direct line.

Just visible on the right of this picture is the line to Weymouth. Note the yellow milepost; behind it can be seen the remains of the embankment on which ran the line enabling southbound trains from Pen Mill to gain direct access to the eastbound LSWR main line.

The old route of the S & D, with its link at Templecombe for Exeter, could have received a major boost to its through passenger traffic had the line remained open. Indeed, the wretchedness of the road links between south-east Dorset and the Bath-Bristol area were, and are, an incentive to find an alternative means of communication, should one be available. It was this that made me suggest to Bob Reid (Sir Robert Reid, Chairman of British Rail) what I have rather grandly styled my proposal for a 'Dorchester Triangle'.

The closure of the S & D, with its initial concept of linking the Bristol and English Channels at Burnham-on-Sea and Poole, had left the only north-south rail links through Wessex as the Bath-Westbury-Salisbury-Southampton line, or the Bath-Westbury-Yeovil-Dorchester-Weymouth line. A glance at the railway map and timetable, however, illustrates the unattractiveness of either for travellers from, say, Poole or Christchurch to Bath or Bristol. One must change either at Dorchester or Southampton. The former entails a walk between the county town's two stations, while the latter means commencing one's journey by heading off miles in the wrong direction; and at neither Dorchester nor Southampton are there linked train connections northwards for the LSWR main line trains. However, if 'my' link were to be built at Dorchester, through trains would again run from Bournemouth to Bath and Bristol, bringing new life and revenue to the precarious Weymouth-Yeovil-Castle Cary route.

In my proposal BR initially showed scant interest. Unwilling to be rebuffed without some resistance, I pressed for more market research into the potential traffic. BR agreed that a link would be useful, but

If my proposed new spur linking the Bournemouth-Weymouth and Yeovil-Weymouth lines at Dorchester is ever built, it could provide a sensible direct link from south-east Dorset to Yeovil, Bath and Bristol, and would fill a gap left by the closure of the Somerset & Dorset Joint Railway.

Local government reorganization, putting parts of Hampshire into Dorset, has profoundly affected commercial and public life, with related consequences for transport requirements.

The 'Dorchester Triangle'

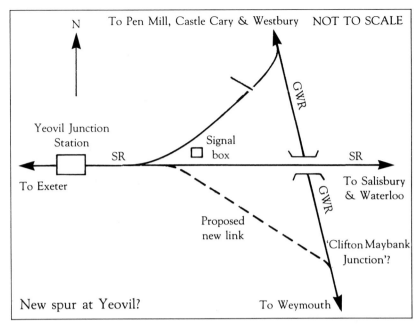

N

To Pen Mill, Castle Cary & Westbury   NOT TO SCALE

GWR

Yeovil Junction
Station

Signal
box

SR

SR

To Exeter

To Salisbury
& Waterloo

GWR

Proposed
new link

'Clifton Maybank
Junction'?

New spur at Yeovil?   To Weymouth

If this link is built, it will improve rail connections and enable BR to save operating costs by concentrating manpower in Yeovil, at Junction station.

on more detailed investigation indicated that an 'inner-town' link would be disruptive in Dorchester, whilst the more feasible 'countryside' link would cost in the region of £6 million and could not be justified. Kenneth Abel, to whom reference was made at the beginning of this chapter, ensured that a survey of potential traffic between south-east Dorset and Avon was conducted, but he felt that it was unlikely to be sufficient to justify the pursuit of my scheme by the County Council. I wonder...

If the Weymouth-Bristol line is to survive, then one new link that may well be built is a new spur into Yeovil Junction station from the Weymouth line which it would leave south of the point where it now runs under the LSWR main line, just to the east of Yeovil Junction signal box. This new link would, as its main purpose, enable BR to close Yeovil Pen Mill Station and to concentrate all Yeovil traffic at the Junction Station. All trains on the north-south line would have to reverse at Yeovil Junction, but as most are diesel multiple units that presumably would be an operational price well worth paying. Perhaps the new junction could be called 'Clifton Maybank Junction' in memory of the goods station of that name. Although originally a transfer point for goods traffic from broad to standard gauge, and open only from 1864 to 1937, the building remained virtually unaltered until 1952 when it was converted into a store. As a relic of broad gauge days it is of historic interest to railway enthusiasts, if to nobody else.

Should the new link be built, then presumably the present section of the Weymouth line between the junction just south of Pen Mill Station to 'Clifton Maybank Junction' would become redundant, would

Western Region three-car diesel multiple unit No 433, forming the 06.00 Bristol Temple Meads to Weymouth train, runs south and prepares to pass under the LSWR main line just to the east of Yeovil Junction box on 1 August 1986.

Immodesty and prejudice combine on sight of this picture to make me revise my opinion that it is impossible to take an interesting railway photograph without a steam engine therein; although one can only contemplate how much more attractive a Churchward 2-6-0 would have looked at the head of this train, the location of which again illustrates the photogenic possibilities hereabouts.

be lifted and would add yet another redundant cutting to the junctions, embankments, cuttings and tracks that, sadly, litter the Somerset & Dorset countryside, unless it was decided to create a 'double track' section from the present parallel but single-line tracks. (Would the mileage posts be altered, I wonder?) Gone too, presumably, would be the fixed distants whose bright yellow faces are such a welcome and familiar landmark to the few people who are fortunate enough to know that stretch of land 'twixt Junction and Pen Mill, the pleasure of which I sampled not once, but twice, in August 1986. The first was pre-planned; the second, on Tuesday 19 August, was certainly not. Yet it was a memorable day. Between the two dates I had visited Hong Kong (twice), Kuala Lumpur and Bangkok, at which last-mentioned place I had found a steam engine still in use as a stationary boiler at Makkasan Works — but that is another tale.

It was the return to Dorset from the Far East on the evening of Monday 18 August that enabled me to profit, in terms of railway enthusiasm, from Western Region's misfortune the following day. Having determined that a day off was in order after some fairly gruelling travelling, I awoke just after 8 am to hear on the radio that 'all train services between Paddington and the West of England are being diverted via Yeovil following a derailment on the main line near Taunton'. Notwithstanding my wife's perverse insistence that I 'must' suffer from jet-lag — which I do not — my mind was immediately filled with thoughts of potentially hectic hours, if not of organized chaos, at Yeovil Junction box, and of unusual motive power on the single-line sections between Castle Cary and Pen Mill and between Pen Mill and Yeovil Junction. Perhaps Jane would accompany me?

Amazingly for August 1986 it was a reasonably sunny day. As the morning wore on, Jane's enthusiasm at the prospect of a visit to 'Railway Yeovil' visibly increased. Having myself previously eulogized the secret terrain between Junction and Pen Mill we (she) decided tht it was 'appropriate' to combine such a visit with a walk with our younger labrador, George. Thus, armed with but one camera (not expecting such a jaunt, my others were in London and being repaired, respectively) we headed west and, after traversing the line at different points between Castle Cary and Yeovil, duly arrived at Yeovil Junction signal box, by prior telephone arrangement, soon after 3 pm that Tuesday afternoon. Jim Maidment was in charge.

Jim Maidment, signalman supreme, surveys his immaculate charge, Yeovil Junction box, in August 1986. Joining the GWR as Temporary Lad Porter at Marston Magna on 13 February 1942, he was steadily promoted: to signalman-porter at Castle Cary in March 1947; to signalman back at Marston Magna later that year; to relief signalman then resident signalman at Yeovil Pen Mill in 1951; to resident signalman — and first in the new box — at Sherborne in October 1955; on relief, based at Yeovil, in 1962; and finally as resident signalman at his present abode in 1969. With 19 years at Junction box and two years to go before retirement, Jim's experience entitles him to that accolade of 'signalman supreme'.

For a railway enthusiast there are few more rewarding occupations than that of listening to the reminiscences of mature and interesting railwaymen. Jim Maidment, like Alan Cox, fits this description well. However, languid, leisurely conversation was not an option that day. Yeovil Junction box, with the paraphernalia of the manual signalling era, and including such niceties as the token for the single-line section 'twixt Junction and Pen Mill, was put to the sword by the day's diversions. Glorious uncertainty — a feature so beloved of enthusiasts in the steam era, and so rarely enjoyed on today's 'plastic railway' — was much in evidence as a stream of HSTs from the Western main line was diverted on to the single-track railway between Yeovil and Castle Cary. To offer a minute-by-minute account of that hectic day might stretch your patience. There is a limit to how far one can enthuse about the numbers of diesel multiple-units, even if they are high-speed trains; the same, frankly, applies, to Class '33' or Class '50' diesel locomotives. Such satisfaction as would be obtained photographically had to do with juxtapositioning of railway features such as Southern semaphore signals adjacent to an HST, or one of these undeniably sleek units at work on a single-track line. The line was originally, as the Wilts, Somerset & Weymouth Railway (WSWR), laid to the broad gauge, so, after conversion to narrow gauge (Castle Cary to Yeovil Pen Mill in 1881), there is ample clearance at the bridges — Castle Cary to Pen Mill was singled on 12 May 1968 — but some limited satisfaction can be obtained, on our increasingly stereotyped railway, from such out-of-course operations.

With the closure of both intermediate stations — Sparkford and Marston Magna — on 3 October 1966, and the deliberate destruction of connections to the Weymouth line from Paddington trains at Castle Cary, it is quite surprising that the line has survived at all. Indeed, many local people in this age of the motor-car, do not know that it still exists. I do not know the logic of closing Sparkford while keeping Chetnole Halt or Yetminster open, although for my part I now use the line whenever possible. Thus journeys from Cardiff or Bristol to Yetminster are reasonably convenient and immeasurably more pleasant than by road. Few rail journeys in England can match the idyllic stretch of line 'twixt Bathampton and Trowbridge, and Brunel's influence hereabouts is still in evidence. (As 1987 closed, semaphores were still in use.) The great man was concerned at the methods employed by the appointed contractors on part of the line, in that they utilized the 'truck' system, whereby payment to the navvies building the line was made in either goods, or tickets which could be exchanged for goods. Shops exchanging tickets for supplies were known to offer poor quality, high prices and short weight, and Brunel was vehemently opposed to this iniquitous system.

The history of the WSWR was fraught with difficulty and with promoting alternative proposals aimed at thwarting rival schemes.

Yeovil featured in both aspects of these developments. In October 1846, representatives of the WSWR met the Board of the GWR when it was proposed to build 100 miles of broad gauge line, including one from Wilton through Shaftesbury, Templecombe and Sherborne to join the WSWR north of Yeovil. It is not difficult to deduce at whom this was aimed.

In 1848, in the wake of national recession, work on the WSWR on both sides of Yeovil was in difficulty: between Frome and Yeovil work was suspended, and little progress was being made southwards from Yeovil to Dorchester. In October 1849, the WSWR directors resolved to sell their line to the GWR, transfer being completed on 14 March 1850 and legalized the following year. As all the WSWR share capital had been spent, an effort to raise money at the local level led to the authorization of the Frome, Yeovil and Weymouth Railway (FYWR). With an authorized capital of £550,000 and borrowing powers of £183,000, the FYWR Act stated that the agreement with the GWR would be void unless the whole of the capital was subscribed within three months. This objective was not achieved, the GWR was forced to raise the cash itself, and thus the scene was set for the rivalry at Yeovil between the GWR and the LSWR. For generations, the two

The embankment of the Yeovil Junction-Yeovil Town line, on which passenger services ceased on 3 October 1966, the line itself closing on 1 March 1967.

This embankment once carried an integral arm of the 'Yeovil Triangle', 'twixt Junction, Town and Pen Mill Stations, on which a shuttle service of push-pull or motor trains operated for generations; one of them can be seen in the picture on page 88. Here, we are looking north-west, where the line from Junction curved around towards Town Station and its junction with the Yeovil-Taunton line. In the right background is Windmill Hill; the line from Pen Mill to Town (and Taunton) ran through the trees below the hill.

GWR takeover: '54xx' Class 0-6-0 pannier tank No 5410 waits at Yeovil Junction, forming the next train to Town. The green station sign proclaims the Southern heritage of the station, in contrast to the livery of the push-pull stock. Note the water-column, the most visible sign of the steam railway. 21 August 1963.

railways and their successors through into BR days, competed for London-Weymouth traffic, Great Western via Castle Cary and Southern via Southampton and Dorchester.

Lest anyone thinks that the 1923 Grouping or 1948 nationalization ended the rivalry between Western and Southern, either here or elsewhere where the systems met, they should think again. Southern men still yearn for the restoration of a full and proper rail service, up from Yeovil Junction to Waterloo and down to Exeter and beyond. When I was there in 1963, one of the perennial changes in regional boundaries put Yeovil into the Western camp. The first act was to remove the most visible Southern presence by replacing the LSWR 'M7' tanks with GWR panniers. That priceless recorder of railway news the *Railway Observer* (RO), journal of the Railway Correspondence and Travel

Society, records in prosaic language changes that were traumatic events indeed for the railwaymen involved. The edition of February 1963 starts the process by recording, under the heading SHED CODE:

'As from 30th December 1962 Exmouth Junction (72A), Yeovil Town (72C), Barnstaple (72E) and Wadebridge (72F) depots were transferred to Western Region, 149 locomotives being involved in the transfer.'

Two editions later, the May *RO* reports in Western Region notes, under the heading YEOVIL TOWN:

'Two auto-fitted panniers, 5410/6, have recently been transferred to Yeovil Town and have replaced the M7s on the push-pull duty to and from Yeovil Junction. On 30th March 5410 was noted on this working with two WR auto trailers. A further two WR

trailers were standing in a siding at Seaton Junction, although on this date an M7 was working the branch with SR stock as usual.' (See page 88).

That last sentence was hardly cause for believing that SR motive power would long survive its railway's take-over by the old enemy. Indeed, the railway itself would be closed down by Brunel & Gooch's successors at the earliest date. The inexorable process was further reported by *RO* the following month, June 1963, under the paragraph heading WEST OF ENGLAND:

'Further to the note in the May *RO* (p 138) it is the intention to employ 64xx pannier tanks on the Seaton branch. On 16th April 6430 duly performed with the two WR trailers, but by 20th April the cars were at Exeter Central for attention and the branch was once more in the hands of an M7 with SR push-pull stock. It is rumoured that the WR has several other jobs in mind for panniers in this area, eg banking at Exeter. 4655/94 are usually to be found sharing the Southern marshalling yard and other freight duties at Exeter with the partially displaced Ws.'

To suggest that the Western always gained the upper hand is almost, but not entirely, true; as I have already mentioned, it was the Southern Region that won the battle for the Weymouth route. As late as 1956, however, a Western Region slip-coach, itself a relic from an earlier age, was 'slipped' from the 'Cornish Riviera' or the 3.30 pm Paddington-Penzance at Heywood Road Junction, Westbury, hauled into Westbury Station and attached to a Bristol-Weymouth semi-fast. Passengers off the 3.30 from Paddington reached Weymouth via Yeovil in 3 hours 27 minutes, compared with 3 hours 31 minutes for the fastest Waterloo-Weymouth train. In addition, Channel Islands boat expresses ran on weekdays from Paddington-Weymouth Quay. But change was in the air.

The last through Paddington to Weymouth Quay Channel Islands Express ran on 26 September 1959, the year after Southern Region took over operating control of the Castle Cary-Weymouth line. Regular Paddington-Weymouth through services ended in 1960. Since then, Western Region has regained control of the line, but it is a haggard shadow of its former self. Yeovil will (probably) never again see express passenger trains from Paddington to Weymouth. All in all, therefore, Yeovil has lost all round. Town Station has gone; so has the line to Taunton. Pen Mill is in effect on a single-track extended branch-line from Westbury rather than a double-track main line with through trains to Paddington. Junction has become nothing more, in truth, than the western end of an extended passing loop on the single-track Salisbury-Exeter line, rather than a four-platform junction and important railhead on the Southern main line from Waterloo to Plymouth and North Cornwall.

What hope is there for an improvement in Yeovil's railway? On the Castle Cary-Weymouth line, the primary task is to prevent closure, although there is no evidence of any immediate threat in spite of critics of the current government's policy. Indeed, I write these words following a meeting with David Mitchell, Minister of State at the Department of Transport with responsibility for railways, whose justifiably proud claim is that more stations have opened than have closed since he assumed his responsibilities. If the Clifton Maybank spur is built, then Yeovil's north-south line will be secure and Yeovil Junction Station will probably get a major face-lift, to compensate for the closure, or reduction to unstaffed station, of Pen Mill.

On the Southern main line, hopes for the introduction of High Speed Trains in 1989 have been dashed. Units displaced from the East Coast Main Line by electrification, once earmarked for Waterloo-Exeter, have been allocated to other BR duties, and the LSWR line is promised — 'threatened' is a better word — upgraded 'Sprinters', in others words DMUs. My ambition still extends to the doubling again of the whole line from Salisbury to Exeter, but that is as yet nothing more than a gleam in my eyes alone, as is my proposed 'Dorchester Triangle' (mentioned on p. 92). Are my dreams just that? To those of use who pleaded and cajoled with Southern Region management for nearly twenty years to reintroduce steam west of Salisbury, their incessant rebuttals made such pleas themselves seem ethereal. Yet 1986 saw new men at the top, fresh ideas and an open-minded attitude to steam, resulting in worthwhile profit and undoubted goodwill for the railway from the 'Blackmore Vale Express'. I am not ashamed to admit to tears in my eyes as *Clan Line* regained her rightful place. One of the 'Blackmore Vale' headboards was replaced by an 'Atlantic Coast Express' on *Clan Line*'s smokebox. As yet, however, Western Region show little sign of encouraging hope for a steam service on the 'triangle' 'twixt Salisbury, Westbury and Yeovil; I shall keep trying. A 'Castle' at Castle Cary would be another triumph. Hopefully between the writing of these words and their subsequent publication my pessimism will have been confounded. I do hope so.

One thing of which we can be sadly certain, however, is that Yeovil Town Station will never reopen, nor will trains run again thence to Taunton via Marston Magna. Yeovil, however, has perhaps against the odds survived — survived Western Region's cruel attempt to close the Southern line west of Salisbury and survived rumoured closures of the Weymouth line. Depending on the outcome of the Local Government Boundary Commission, the town may finally have no station at all in Somerset, but Yeovil's railway service seems secure if not yet set fair to improve. The semaphore signals will in due course go, but the fleeting glimpse of an HST service has been dashed by BR's change of mind about those units displaced by the ECML electrification. My Parliamentary colleagues and I will keep a suspicious eye on developments; it is too soon to decide whether to regard the future with hope or despair.

Sometimes constituents unearth interesting items for me! This old notice refers to Yeovil Town station, and my acquisition of it is described opposite.

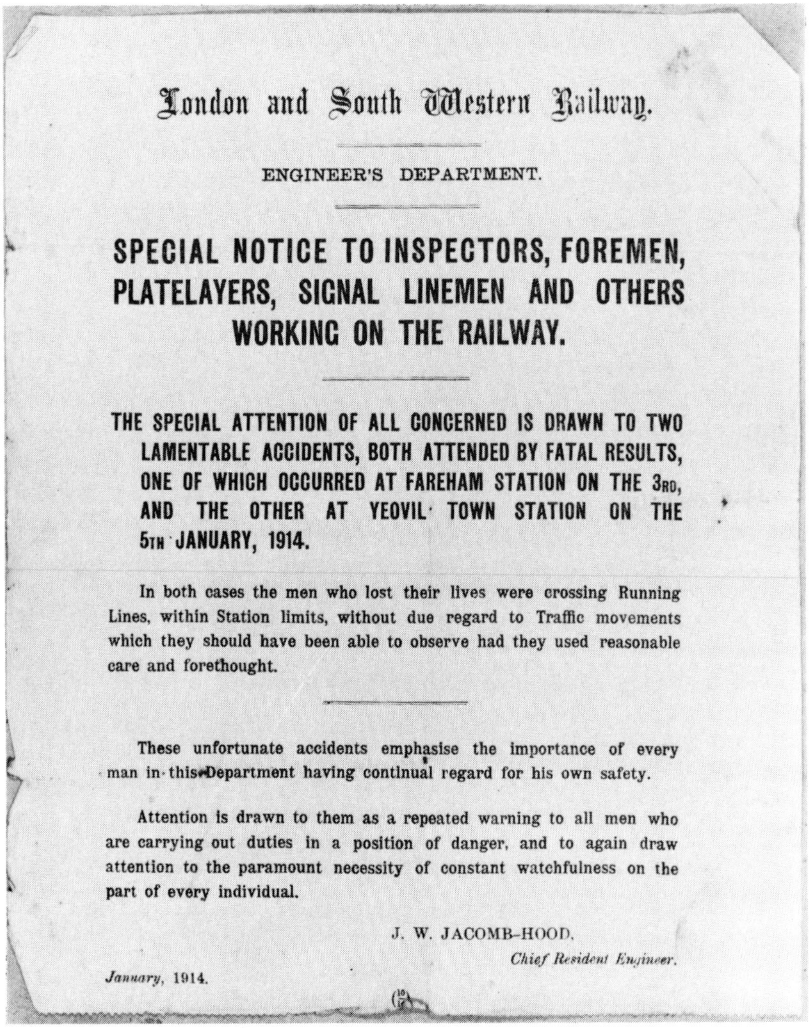

London and South Western Railway.

ENGINEER'S DEPARTMENT.

SPECIAL NOTICE TO INSPECTORS, FOREMEN, PLATELAYERS, SIGNAL LINEMEN AND OTHERS WORKING ON THE RAILWAY.

THE SPECIAL ATTENTION OF ALL CONCERNED IS DRAWN TO TWO LAMENTABLE ACCIDENTS, BOTH ATTENDED BY FATAL RESULTS, ONE OF WHICH OCCURRED AT FAREHAM STATION ON THE 3RD, AND THE OTHER AT YEOVIL TOWN STATION ON THE 5TH JANUARY, 1914.

In both cases the men who lost their lives were crossing Running Lines, within Station limits, without due regard to Traffic movements which they should have been able to observe had they used reasonable care and forethought.

These unfortunate accidents emphasise the importance of every man in this Department having continual regard for his own safety.

Attention is drawn to them as a repeated warning to all men who are carrying out duties in a position of danger, and to again draw attention to the paramount necessity of constant watchfulness on the part of every individual.

J. W. JACOMB-HOOD.

Chief Resident Engineer.

January, 1914.

One of the many privileges and advantages of being both a railway enthusiast and Member of Parliament is that people come to know of one's interest, and proffer items of railway interest which might otherwise be consigned to scrap-heap or dustbin. Sometimes these might be more suitable receptacles, and sometimes people imagine they have treasures beyond price for which they anticipate rich rewards. With, sadly, many miles of closed and lifted railway in East Dorset, diverse items appear from time to time. Once I acquired an LSWR boundary post at a Conservative Party branch function, leaving discreetly to dig it up away at the bottom of my host's garden.

On Friday 13 February 1987, my constituents Gordon and Jill Nash handed me an interesting pile of mouldering papers from the early years of the century, all connected with the LSWR. Having purchased part of the trackbed of the erstwhile line between Wimborne and West Moors, they take an interest in the history of the line. From an ailing neighbour they collected the papers to which I referred, amongst which is the notice illustrated opposite; it is included here because one of the two fatal accidents to which it relates occurred at Yeovil Town Station. If that is seemingly insufficient reason so to digress, then look at the identity of the LSWR's Chief Resident Engineer, in whose name the notice was issued; J. W. Jacomb-Hood was the great great uncle of Gillian Jacomb-Hood, the very first secretary whom I was able only half to employ on being elected Member of Parliament in 1970.

Other interesting notes and notices include reports of fires on the line in the Wimborne and Ringwood areas; the land owned by Lord Normanton at Summerly seems frequently to have been thus afflicted. There is an interesting sheet of notes, presumably an appendix to the working timetable and dated 15 October 1914, referring to a number of special trains, including the following:

(1) Troops, 2 Officers, 750 Men, Norwich to Swanage
(2) Military horses to Southampton West

On the basis that 'Dorset' is included in this chapter, I refer to this material, totally unrelated to Yeovil, but addressed to the 'Foreman Loco Dept Bournemouth Central'. As Bournemouth *was* in Hampshire, but is now in Dorset, and as my hook on which to hang this chapter was Local Government reorganization, this seems both the time and the place at which to stop.

Perhaps *Somerset* would like Bournemouth...

10A, 10D, 10F

Covering my tracks, at the very end of steam, meant three places: Burnley, Preston and Carnforth, or in railway terminology, the Motive Power Depots at Rose Grove (10F), Lostock Hall (10D) and Carnforth (10A). These were the last three BR steam sheds to close. In a book unashamedly fuelled by nostalgia, containing previously-unpublished colour photographs, and seeking regionally to balance the bias created by chapters featuring Yeovil and Highbridge, it seems right and sensible to devote a chapter to a small corner of England that perhaps inadvertently has written itself into the history books. These three sheds, and the role they filled in July and just into August 1968, ensures for them memorials, memories and tributes which, in purely historic terms, they may not merit.

It would be comparatively simple to write a tome detailing the railway developments at Preston, Burnley and Carnforth. Preston, with Bolton, Wigan and Warrington, was an early 'railway town', the railway having arrived in Preston by 1831, and the town being linked by 1838 to the Liverpool & Manchester Railway. The Preston & Wigan Railway, through its alliance with the Wigan Branch Railway, was a partner in the very first railway amalgamation sanctioned by Parliament. That amalgamation created the North Union (see the map opposite), which itself took a pivotal role in what, today, we call the West Coast Main Line. Unlike the towns created by the railway — Crewe or Swindon — Preston was an old town given a new role, an added importance, as a railway junction.

Let me stop here and now. History, for the purpose of this chapter, lasted but three years: from 6 August 1965, when I took my first photograph at Preston, to 31 July 1968, when my whole day was devoted to recording the last week of working steam on Britain's national railway system. My photography at Preston on that first visit actually comprised photographs from the cab of a 'Peak' diesel in which I was fortunate enough to travel from Glasgow to Preston. I was *en route* to Liverpool and thence across the Mersey to Birkenhead where I was Prospective Conservative Parliamentary Candidate. At Preston, the kind driver who had allowed me to accompany him from Glasgow relinquished charge of his steed, so I disembarked and managed a couple more shots of steam at work at Preston before we pulled away for the last leg of that journey, with me in the train.

That brief dissertation about Preston station was brought about by

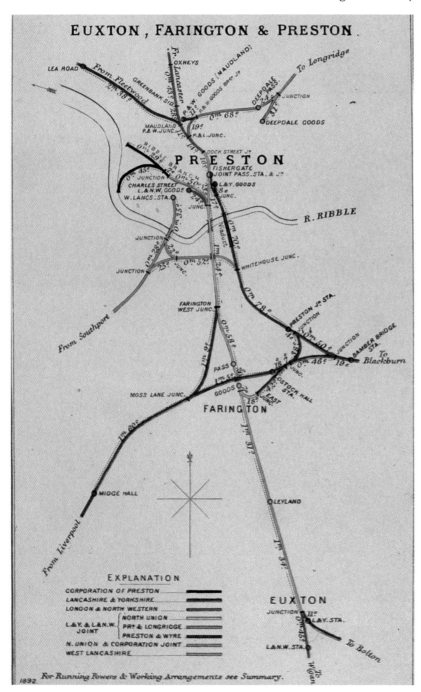

Lostock Hall and Farington, as well as Preston itself, contain a maze of railway junctions; the major lines survive. For a stranger, as was I, visiting the area fleetingly in search of steam, it was not always easy to identify one's precise location.

In fact, further junctions were created in later years than the 1888 situation shown here. The main north-south line is, of course, the West Coast Main Line through Preston. It flourishes, and the lines from Preston to Fleetwood ('Blackpool' would be on today's map), to Liverpool and to Blackburn are in situ. The Southport line has gone, as has the Longridge branch, as well as much of Preston's own immediate rail network.

Previous page *Enthusiasts in droves descended on Lostock Hall and Rose Grove at the end of steam, and volunteers willingly kept clean the surviving engines. Here at Lostock Hall on 25 June 1968, 'Black Five' No 45305, lined-out, stands out of steam at the back of Lostock Hall, her home shed. By this date, shed and number plates had gone, but painted detail confirmed that somebody cared and was determined to see that the survivors ended their days in dignity. No 45305 subsequently survived into preservation.*

the memory of my first railway photography there, but Lostock Hall shed, of course, was not in Preston town in any case. Preston had its own, LNWR, shed, opened by the abovementioned North Union Railway as early as 1838. I say 'its own' guardedly, as the early history of Preston shed is confusing historically and in any case no real part of this brief tale. The North Union became part of the LNWR which became part of the LMS which became part of BR. Over the years it was shuffled about administratively, subject to a ravaging fire in 1961 and closed soon afterwards, on 12 September that year; its allocation was dispersed to Lostock Hall, to Carnforth and to Warrington.

Lostock Hall meanwhile, a Lancashire & Yorkshire establishment, opened in 1882, thus enabling the L & Y to terminate its arrangement to stable some of its engines at the nearby LNWR shed at Preston. Lostock Hall was coded 24C, under Accrington, by the LMS in May 1946, nearby Preston being coded 24K, also under Accrington, in 1958. Whilst Preston had already gone, Lostock Hall survived to be re-coded 10D by BR from September 1963. Having taken over both locomotives and duties from Preston shed, there were frequently in excess of fifty engines in steam at the turn of the years 1966/67, mainly '8F's and 'Black Fives'. Lostock Hall became a famed location for steam enthusiasts into 1968, the shed finally closing, much mourned, on 5 August in that year. Lostock Hall was near Farington, the meeting place of LNWR and Lancashire & Yorkshire territory to the south of Preston, and halfway between the town and Euxton Junction, where the lines to Bolton and Manchester diverge from the WCML which continues southwards to Wigan, Crewe and eventually Euston.

As Lostock Hall was associated with, but not part of, Preston, so was Rose Grove in relationship to Burnley. The latter town, however, in pure railway terms, was monopolized by a single company, the Lancashire & Yorkshire, thus never really assuming importance. The pre-grouping 'motor trains' that ran between Rose Grove and Colne via Burnley Barracks and Burnley (Bank Top) survive as second-class-only trains from Blackburn to Colne in Table 108 of BR's timetable to May 1987. (However, in the October 1987 to May 1988 timetable, the 'second class only' tag has been deleted.) Some trains start at Preston and run to Colne; some Preston trains run Preston-Blackburn-Accrington-Rose Grove and into Yorkshire, terminating at Leeds; gone, however, are the trains through Rose Grove as part of the service from Manchester Victoria to Skipton. Indeed, where once the railway pioneers strode across mountains to join the counties of Lancaster and York, our modern railway masters, by truncating lines such as Colne-Skipton, have recreated the barriers. Rose Grove shed itself, with its proximity to the high moors, exuded bleakness and isolation in keeping with the mood of depression and despair that attended the end of steam in the land of its birth when I took my last photograph there as the sun set on 31 July 1968. The poignancy of that moment is more

memorable than the quality of the photograph in the fading light. Fast colour film today is taken for granted, but in those days a steady hand was necessary at sunset.

Rose Grove shed itself opened some fifteen years after its L & Y fellow-depot Lostock Hall, in 1899. Alongside Rose Grove Station, its duties were essentially freight and mainly coal, nearby Accrington and Colne depots handling most of the local passenger duties. Colne depot's closure, in 1936, saw Rose Grove receive passenger tank engines for the duties thus acquired. In its LMS days it, too, was under Accrington administratively, being coded 24B; in the 1963 BR re-organization it became 10F, which it retained until it, too, joined Lostock Hall in the final trio of BR steam sheds to succumb. By the end, only Stanier '8F's and 'Black Fives' remained here too on that closure day, 5 August 1968.

The last of the trio of final active sheds, Carnforth, has mercifully survived to provide us with the nearest one can get, *via* preservation, to the atmosphere of a real engine shed, although even my affection and admiration for my friends at Steamtown will not permit me to romanticize into an equation between a handful of gleaming and cossetted 'Pacifics' and other preserved locomotives, and the workaday scenes that I enjoyed there on 25 June 1968. Unsurprisingly at that date, LMS 'Black Fives' and '8F's predominated, but BR Standard '4' 4-6-0 No 75048 was photographed heading a freight towards Barrow as it passed the motive power depot. 75048 was one of the ten members of the class at work survived into 1968, being transferred to Carnforth

With cabside number visibly cleaned, 'Black Five' 4-6-0 No 45196 blasts under the road bridge by Rose Grove station, with the yard in the background. The driver looks at the camera: it is a gloomy day, 10 December 1965, and as yet Rose Grove's destiny as one of the last three steam sheds is an unknown future event. Note the engine's home shed painted on the buffer beam, the shunting semaphore signals, and that poignant sight of smoke hanging under a bridge in dank winter weather.

Carnforth's turntable revolves at the behest of steam power supplied by its 'host' locomotive, 'Black Five' No 44874, under the watchful eye of the fireman on 25 June 1968. She survived to the very end of BR steam six weeks later, and was scrapped at Draper's, Hull, in March 1969. This photograph perhaps epitomizes the difference, and indeed the very different appeal, of the real railway, with filthy engine, missing shedplate and forlorn young railwayman, compared to the spotless jollity of the preservation scene.

from Lostock Hall in June '67, and withdrawn as one of the final surviving members of the class in August 1968. Also on shed and photographed were Nos 75019/20, from the same class, the former still on shed and due to survive into August, whilst 75020, although officially not withdrawn, was already on the scrap-line. It sported an 8K (Bank Hall) shedplate. Also on shed were three engines destined for preservation. Perhaps it is worth listing the motive power photographed on the shed and on duty at Carnforth that day:

LMS 'Black Five' 4-6-0: 44758, 44874, 44963, 45025, 45095.
LMS '8F' 2-8-0: 48062, 48167, 48765.
LMS '4' 2-6-4T (Fairburn): 42085.
LNER 'B1' 4-6-0: 61306.
BR Standard '4' 4-6-0: 75019, 75020, 75048.
BR '9F' 2-10-0: 92223.
BR Standard 'Britannia' 4-6-2: 70013.

Where Lostock Hall and Rose Grove were essentially freight-orientated, Carnforth, by the nature of its railway heritage, was at the hub of a system comprising not only the LNWR but also the Midland and the Furness Railways. In the early years, all three companies maintained engine sheds at this important junction; not surprisingly, the LMS, into which all three constituent companies were placed by the 1923 Grouping, combined the three sheds into one modern depot in a scheme drawn up in 1938. With wartime priorities, completion of the scheme was delayed until the new depot finally opened in December 1944. Coded 24L in February 1958, it was re-coded by BR in September 1963, becoming 10A and thus completing the trio for this chapter's title. As with Lostock Hall and Rose Grove, it closed on 5 August 1968.

If in 1987 the survival of the line to Colne from Rose Grove is an agreeable surprise, then the shape of the current railway map around Carnforth is even more so, although West Coast Main Line trains no longer stop there. The platforms serve only trains on the Barrow line or the infrequent but still existing Leeds to Morecambe service, a real

Unlike Rose Grove and Lostock Hall, Carnforth was not part of industrial Lancashire, being essentially a small town where the railway was itself of significance by its junction status acquired through geography. With the Furness Hills beckoning, BR Standard '4' 4-6-0 No 75048 heads from the yard on to the Barrow line on 25 June 1968. Note the crane, signal gantry, signal box roof and, in the far left of the picture, lines of withdrawn steam engines.

hangover from the pre-grouping days of the Midland Railway. Carnforth was the point where trains from Barrow on the Furness Railway met the WCML, the connection being made in 1857. This connection was of considerable value to Barrow's output of iron ore and subsequently of the local haematite ore, necessary in the manufacture of steel. In the other direction, the line over Stainmore from the Durham coalfield enabled coking coal from the north-east to reach

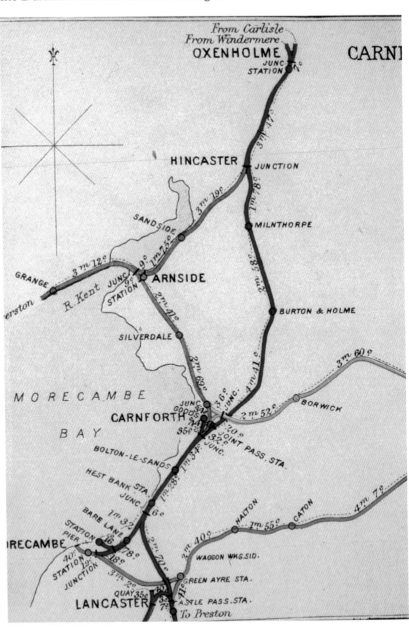

Carnforth's inter-company junction status is clearly shown here. The grey line is that of the Furness Railway, to Ulverston and Barrow; the red is that of the London & North Western Railway, mainly the West Coast Main Line; the green is the Midland Railway's line to Leeds; and the yellow is the Furness & Midland Joint line, linking Carnforth and Wennington. In the immediate vicinity of Carnforth, the main line system remains intact. A small town owing its significance to the railway, Carnforth's key junction status can be seen here. The line to Barrow features in the photograph on page 111.

the furnaces of Furness. A comparison of some of the Leeds to Morecambe services in 1922 and 1987 is instructive:

		1922			1987		
Depart	Leeds	08.02	10.28	15.15	08.26	10.24	15.24
Arrive	Morecambe	11.48	12.56	18.05	10.53	13.05	17.50

The frequency of the service in the year before grouping far surpassed that available today, and that chilling phrase in recent timetables 'Second Class only unless otherwise shown' leaves little to the imagination when seeking to compare the comfort offered by Midland Railway 1922 with British Rail 1987. In 1988, the service is, however, improved — a harbinger of better times again? I have never been to Barrow-in-Furness, but have always been fascinated by the history of the railway thereabouts; it epitomizes the unique character of each of the varied parts of our island.

10A, 10D, 10F: Carnforth, Lostock Hall and Rose Grove. Hardly the most glamorous trio of sheds, yet in those last hectic weeks of steam twenty years ago an army of enthusiasts descended on them from all corners of Britain. Filthy, neglected engines, working literally until they

'Twixt Preston and Blackburn lies some pleasant countryside, through which the afternoon (17.38) freight passes, at Mintholme on 31 July 1968. The engine — '8F' 2-8-0 No 48340 — is filthy beyond description, but this was the steam railway in its final week, as we remember . . .

In those final few months, this engine, like a lost soul, was transferred from Northwich to Rose Grove (March '68); to Bolton (April); to Rose Grove again (July); and survived the final weeks until steam's demise. She was cut up in December 1968 by Ward's at Beighton, Sheffield.

*Farington, south of Preston,
contains a wealth of junctions
and triangles, by the Grouping
even more extensive than shown
on the map on page 105.
Rounding the sharp east-to-north
curve marked as 38 chains long
on the map, comes an
unidentified '8F' 2-8-0 with an
engineer's train on 4 June 1968.
It was an excellent area for
railway photography, but rarely
seems to be featured.*

ground to a halt, were cleaned and polished by fervent admirers of
those mundane Stanier workhorses that saw out the last few diagrams.
For me such enforced companionship was totally undesirable. Solitude
is a prerequisite of enjoyment of my chosen hobby and inevitably the
conglomeration of large numbers of people in a confined space is
anathema. However, if it seemed overcrowded at Lostock Hall, today's
steam happenings are as Armageddon compared to those days. In any
case, within the area of the L-shape made out by the railway joining
the three sheds was much open countryside, and I recall particularly
Mintholme Crossing, on the L & Y Blackburn to Preston line between
Hoghton and Bamber Bridge.

The temptation to trespass beyond the confines of the shed was
considerable, particularly at Lostock Hall where numerous freight-only
lines and junctions created opportunities for photography. The sharp

curves at the point where southbound trains from Preston gain the Blackburn line at Farington enable me to recall a series of shots of an unidentified '8F' rounding the line on an embankment; and Farington East Junction and the freight-only line to Leyland provided photogenic signals and signal boxes as background.

At Rose Grove I recall '8F's struggling to haul heavy freights out of the sidings, and the willow-herb on the bank at the junction of the Padiham branch. Steeply-graded, the coal trains were braked hard as they took the branch. Then there was Burnley Central Station, with its backdrop of Lowry-like mills and industrial buildings, so in keeping with this part of north-east Lancashire.

So steam died — in Lancashire where it saw its early flowering. Those of us who were there will never forget Carnforth, Rose Grove and Lostock Hall.

TURKISH DELIGHT

There comes a time when one accepts that one's sheets have been slept in, and one's towels used, by others who have gone before, and one wonders who they were. As we left the Railway Works Guest House of Turkish Railways (TCDD) at Sivas, Jane and I noticed simply that the towels which we had removed from the cupboard and used had been neatly refolded and returned to await the next guest.

To mention this trivial detail of one's travel experiences in Turkey is not to cast aspersions on the hospitality; quite the reverse, for we were treated as honoured guests at Sivas. It is, however, proper to point out that searching for steam in Turkey, in its declining years, requires a willingness to sacrifice creature comforts. In my hectic life, railway-related activities are necessarily restricted. Other facets of one's life — family, politics, business — make strident calls, so family holiday travel to Turkey was a prerequisite to a week in search of steam with my long-suffering bride.

Turkey, like many of the remaining countries where steam lingers on the national railway system, shuns those whose passion for this form of motive power is matched only by our disdain for diesel or electric machinery. Indeed, only China seems sufficiently mature and self-confident of itself in its willingness to welcome steam railway enthusiasts. Their attitude is increasingly rewarded by an upsurge of railway tourism. In sharp contradistinction, the police and military authorities in Turkey are often far from friendly to the 'long-lens brigade' of railway photographers. There must be a moral or a conclusion to be drawn from the fact that in the People's Republic we are welcome while in NATO Turkey it can be very different; whilst in the Soviet Union all the steam-engines still at work are figments of the imagination of western enthusiasts obviously assumed to be engaged in espionage! However, this chapter is about my travels in Turkey, a country where it undoubtedly helps if as a railway enthusiast one is also a British Member of Parliament. My thanks, therefore, to HE Rahmi Gumrukcuoglu, the Turkish Ambassador in London, for providing me with a letter, in Turkish naturally, of the 'To Whom It May Concern' variety.

I am by nature rather lazy. Where others have toiled, researched, travelled and recounted their experiences, I have latched, often late in the day, on to their coat-tails. Thus in 1985, having gleaned information particularly from the pages of *Continental Railway Journal (CRJ)*, I 'escaped' from a day on the beach and headed, firstly inland and then for Izmir. Good fortune rather than good reconnaissance rewarded my efforts, but even by this date steam on the line was becoming rare and hard to find. Requests for local information from railway officials about steam sometimes produced straightforward and presumably deliberate misinformation. However, I was by sheer luck able to capture one half-steam-hauled train; a doubled-headed 'express' with, unfortunately, the diesel at its head.

The banker at Camlik was still a simmering steam-engine, dozing in the hot sunshine, the driver proudly displaying colour prints taken and sent to him by British and West German visitors. The main 'target' of the day, however, was Izmir's Alsancak shed. On arrival, it was not long before I realized that my 'To Whom It May Concern' letter was not an 'open sesame'. 'Unless I have a copy of the letter on my desk, no letters are valid as far as I am concerned,' was the implausible and unhelpful response to my epistle from the Turkish Ambassador. Back and forth from shed to General Manager's office in the station, a mixture of persuasion and bluster, and finally I gained entry to the shed with my camera.

I was told that the shed would close to steam at the end of the year, in just over three months' time. I was told quite categorically that Halkapinar Works in Izmir was already closed. Officially, all steam operation ended in Turkey on 31 December 1985. It did not. Don't believe TCDD; obtain your information from *CRJ*. Likewise, the only reliable reference book about Turkish steam comes from the enthusiasts' bible for the country — a book on the shelves of men like Ibrahim Yasan, the Works Manager at Sivas Works. The title of the bible is *Steam in Turkey*; the author, Ted Talbot.

Since my railway photography began, in November 1962, it has always been both necessary and desirable to mould my chosen hobby around the cast of my life. A few days after that day in September 1985 spent chasing steam to Izmir, Jane and I found ourselves on another Turkish beach, where a chance meeting with a charming couple led in unlikely fashion to 'Steam 86', our beach friends agreeing to chase steam with us for a week the following year. During the ensuing months I sent numerous cuttings from *CRJ* and the various monthly magazines, we spoke on the phone on a few occasions, and arranged to meet in Ankara. Thus, from a chance meeting on the beach in September 1985, Jane and I stepped expectantly off a plane at Ankara Airport one Tuesday evening in September 1986. Our once-met friend Canip Orhun was there to meet us and within an hour we were dining with him and his wife Ceyda, their son Cem and English daughter-in-law. Cem works in the office of the Turkish Prime Minister, and

Overleaf German-built 'Austerity' 2-10-0s of Deutsche Reichsbahn (DRB) Class '52' — known as the 'Kriegslok' locomotives — were initially hired, and later acquired, by TCDD. Here, one of the Borsig engines, No 56514 built in 1943, simmers quietly on Izmir Alcancak shed on 10 September 1985. Another member of the class stands out of steam on the right.

Two years after the official 'end of steam' on TCDD, steam engines were still being given major overhauls at Halkapinar Works, Izmir.

thus the following night we found ourselves in Sivas, guests of TCDD at Sivas Works Guest House. The search for Turkish steam '86 had begun — and for me, if not for Jane, the antecedence of the users of those Guest House towels was of no real concern.

This is a railway book, not an account of the travels of Robert and Jane Adley. Let me therefore spare you the gazettering aspects of our journey. That all work on steam locomotive repairs at Sivas has ended is herewith duly confirmed. That no more steam locomotives were at work at Sivas turned out not to be accurate, although the Skoda Standard 2-10-0 No 56156 working in the yards was bereft of number plate, was restricted to a short stretch of track and was described to me as 'not a locomotive any more, merely a mobile steam-heating boiler'.

One of the primary targets of my search for steam was a British '8F' 2-8-0 in service. Such information as was available led me to believe that Erzincan was the place to find one; that the area based on Erzerum was amongst the last steam strongholds on a main line; and that the incongruous three-pronged branches to Burdur, Isparta and Eğridir survived as an isolated system still not penetrated by the dreaded diesel. From the Mediterranean fastness of Side, therefore, my initial foray was planned. Not for the first time, luck played a not inconsiderable part in determining my fortunes. Temporarily 'allocated' to the Avis office in Side was a man who lived in Eğridir, who spoke some English and who was willing to act as driver/guide for the day. Having also enrolled Arthur Baumgartner, a Swiss banker staying at the same hotel in Side, to the 'Brotherhood of Steam', the three of us set off at 5.10 am in the general direction of Burdur, Isparta and Eğridir.

Embarking on an excursion fraught with uncertainty about the reception that awaits, as well as the likelihood of rewards for one's search, is an exhilarating prospect. Railway enthusiasts in Turkey 'caught' photographing around stations and motive power installations have reported varied receptions, from friendly welcome through unhelpful refusal to camera confiscation, arrest, imprisonment and deportation. Armed with my Ambassadorial epistle, silky smile and Turkish driver/guide we headed west, skirted around Antalya as the sun came up, turned north through the mountains and decided to head first for Burdur, then Isparta, and finally Eğridir. Without the basic knowledge or indeed possession of *Yolcu Rehberi*, the TCDD timetable, let alone adequate reconnaissance, it was little more than miraculous to arrive at Burdur Station just before 8 am and to be told that the morning arrival from Eğridir was due very shortly. Whilst I encumbered myself with cameras, tripod, case and notebook, hoping vainly to pass unnoticed amongst the locals, my driver/guide was seeking permission for me to take photographs.

At Burdur, that exhilaration to which I referred earlier was given tangible and visible vent by the proximity of the motive power depot

Opposite *Self-evidently of British lineage, 2-8-2 No 46103, built by Robert Stephenson & Co Ltd in 1929, stands by the turntable at what is euphemistically termed the 'museum' at Izmir Alcancak, on 10 September 1985. At the date of entry into service, the class was acquired by the Aydin Railway, which was the correct name of the Ottoman Railway Company — ORC.*

to the station's only platform. Pending the delivery of glad or ill tidings,
I decided to capture as many pictures as possible from the platform.
Tantalizingly, the sign 'TCDD LOCOMOTIF DEPOT' beckoned
seductively a mere 200 yards away. A locomotive simmered smokily
in the middle distance; the sun rose steadily, its colour yellowing as
the gap between it and the mountains diminished. Suddenly happiness
arrived — it was in order for me to take pictures. I was welcome at
the engine shed, and the train from Eğridir hove into view, albeit tender

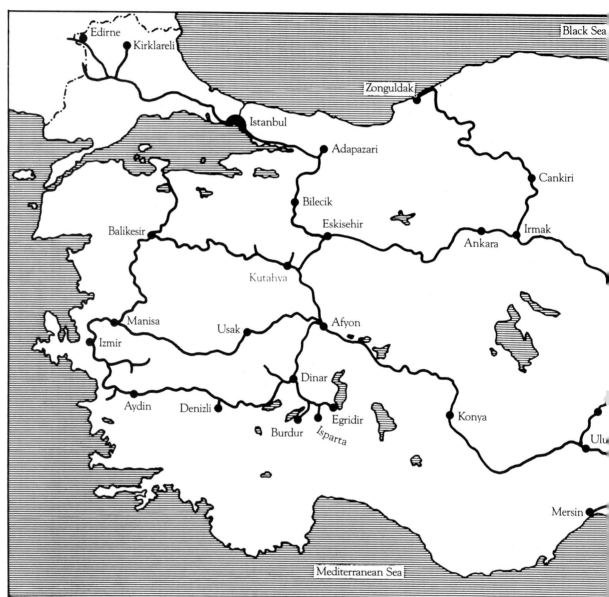

first and hauled by a Standard 2-10-0.

As interest in Turkish motive power is, even now, somewhat esoteric, there seems little point in regaling you with too much detail about the numbers of the engines seen and photographed, nor in providing a breakdown of the detailed differences between the various types of TCDD Standard 2-10-0. At Burdur, however, on the day of my visit, there were still two of the splendid Prussian 'G8' Class 0-8-0s in steam. One, indeed, was active on shunting and pilot duties for two hours

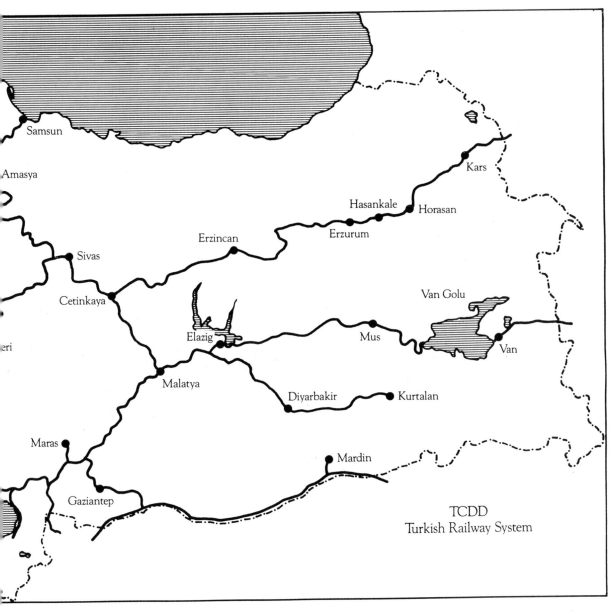

TCDD
Turkish Railway System

Previous page Burdur shed is
the motive power depot serving
the isolated Burdur-Isparta-
Egridir system, still 100 per cent
steam at the time of writing.
Here, on 11 September 1986, the
small but active shed hosts, on
the left, class 'G8' 0-8-0 No
44055, alongside Henschel-built
'Kriegslok' 2-10-0 No 56503.
The 'G8' was one of the oldest,
and certainly one of the most
interesting, engines still active in
Turkey. The class was originally
introduced by the Prussian State
Railways, and No 44055 is one
of a batch of ten 'G8s' built new
in 1924 for the Smyrna-Cassaba
Railway, one of the constituent
companies of TCDD. She had
recently been overhauled at the
officially closed Halkapinar
Works.

Opposite The quality of coal
utilized by TCDD advertises
itself through the chimney of
Prussian 'G8' Class 0-8-0 No
44055, resting between duties on
Burdur shed on 11 September
1986. Note the shed doors and
the tackle.

at Burdur yard and station. Enquiry revealed that it had only recently returned to Burdur from overhaul at Halkapinar Works, Izmir, the self-same works that had, so I was assured, already closed at the time of my visit to Izmir a year previously...

Presumably reacting in accordance with 'standing orders', Burdur's shedmaster, Huseyn Erçelik, welcomed me warmly, saying that I could wander at will around his depot, but indicating that I should not photograph any locomotive undergoing repairs. It seemed that he felt he had to make some restrictions — but as no locomotives appeared to be undergoing repairs, as opposed to receiving normal shed attention, this 'restriction' presented no difficulty.

Most practitioners of the art or profession of railway photography are sufficiently organized, determined and thorough as to be accustomed to travelling to a particular place, at a pre-ordained time, to take that 'special' photograph. Even had I these worthy attributes it still remains unlikely, nowadays, that my life, with its numerous constraints, could permit of any such luxury. There is also the other factor in this equation, namely that familiarity breeds contempt. Ask any of the editors of the railway journals and they will tell you they are inundated with material from preserved steam main-line outings at predictable and well-known locations. Further afield, the number of cameramen will be thinner; the distances are greater, and thus the likelihood of queueing for the best pitch or falling over one's fellow-enthusiasts less likely a hazard. In Turkey there is the added unpredictability of the timetable to add spice to any such venture.

Few places, in this day and age, appeal to me sufficiently to warrant a long journey for the purpose of photographing one single train. However, Ted Talbot's excellent tome *Steam in Turkey*, without which no railway enthusiast should visit the country, contains one particular black-and-white photograph that, through its historic site in relation to the country's railway history combined with its scenic attraction, finally persuaded me to allocate half a day with the limited end-product of one photographic destination. The place was Eğridir, and the site the iron girder bridge on the lengthy haul up from the station. With the lake in the background and the locomotive working hard up the grade from a standing start, the journey to Eğridir seemed an adventure worth contemplating, notwithstanding that journey's end was a very long way from Side where we were based.

There was, however, time for an excellent lunch in Isparta, marred only slightly by the lack of consideration of the other patrons at the restaurant for a small tortoise whose ambitions were limited to a lunchtime stroll. In mid-afternoon we arrived at Eğridir. The approach to the town from the west is breath-taking. Rounding a bend up in the hills, the azure blue lake, sparkling in September sunshine, suddenly appears ahead of you, replacing the dun-coloured uniformity of the mountains. As the road rounds the bend it crosses the single-track

Train No 1402, the 06.30 from Isparta, has just arrived at Burdur on 11 September 1986, hauled tender-first by 'Kriegslok' 2-10-0 No 56503. My tripod stands 'unattended' on the platform at this all-steam location whose few foreign 'tourists' include the occasional railway enthusiast. The low early morning sun is evident by the long shadows. These Second-World-War-built engines are kept in excellent external condition by Burdur shed.

railway line in the cutting below. At Burdur some hours earlier, I had ascertained that the evening train, undoubtedly steam-hauled, was scheduled to depart Eğridir at 18.00; the first view of the lake determined me to choose my photographic location and then enjoy a swim, before seeking to create my masterpiece on colour film.

The first potential hazard, on descending into the small town, was to notice that the place was crawling with military personnel, whilst shellfire reverberated around the hills encompassing this remote town. Brazen overt ostentation rather than nervous hesitant furtiveness paid off, as so often happens. When in doubt, set up your tripod — don't hide. This was my tactic once we had found the station, itself no easy task. There is little resemblance between the Eğridir branch — for that is what it is, notwithstanding its origins in the development of the Turkish railway system — and its rural British counterpart. Eğridir Station is hidden shyly away, virtually invisible from the road. It was the wisps of steam rising from slumbering Kriegslok 2-10-0 No 56550 that gave us our first visual evidence of the existence of the railway. In the warmth of an autumn afternoon, hours of simmering inactivity seemed more appropriate for an ancient 0-4-4 tank then for a massive modern ten-coupled machine at this somnolent spot.

Eğridir's location as a terminus on Turkey's railway map would seem incongruous indeed to those unfamiliar with the historic background. Turkey in the middle of the nineteenth century found itself as a competitive battleground on which the competing European powers sought to increase their influence through railway developments. Of these, the Ottoman Railway Company (ORC), obtaining their concession on 22 September 1856, opened their first section, from Izmir to Seydiköy, on 30 October 1858; this was the first railway in the Ottoman Empire. Expansion of the ORC continued spasmodically, pressing on eastwards and throwing off a number of branches. Progress towards the ultimate destination of Konya, for connection with the line to Baghdad, took another step with the completion of a further sixty miles, from Dinar to Eğridir, on 1 November 1912.

By now, the political climate in Turkey was very different from that existing during the early years of the ORC. Permission was sought in 1914 to extend the ORC's line eastwards again from Eğridir to Konya, where connection could be made with the Anatolian Railway — known as CFOA (Societé du Chemin de fer Ottoman d'Anatolie), a German-backed company. The CFOA, in the light of the increasingly close relationship between Turkey and Germany, had been granted permission in 1893 to extend their railway line from Ankara eastwards to Kayseri, Sivas and eventually on to Baghdad, but with a branch from Eskişehir west of Ankara, southwards to Konya, the latter line being completed first at the request of the Sultan. When completed, Konya then became the railhead, but the line thence eastwards made no progress prior to the First World War. Lest I become bogged down in an attempt to write a *précis* of Turkish railway history, let alone of Turkey's political background, let it suffice to say that the ORC were refused permission in 1914 to extend eastwards; the Ottoman government vetoed the scheme since it favoured the German-backed Baghdad Railway. Thus it was that the Turkish-German alliance resulted in Eğridir becoming an unlikely railway terminus.

Eğridir with its lake is a beautiful but remote place. Indeed, the sixty miles of line through mountainous country from Dinar took six years to build. It was with a feeling of satisfaction therefore that we had reached our destination. A further inspection of the author's photograph on page 9 of Ted Talbot's *Steam in Turkey* enabled me to direct my attention towards finding 'the bridge at Eğridir'. This presented no difficulty. With nearly three hours before the 18.00 departure, Arthur Baumgartner and I decided to try the waters of the lake. This necessitated my purchasing a pair of trunks in the town. Happily not yet on the foreign tourist trail, and for Turks the end of the season, for an expenditure of little more than £1 I obtained the necessary attire which, whilst lacking elegance, nevertheless fulfilled its purpose.

We enjoyed our swim in Lake Eğridir. At about 5.15 we went to

Overleaf It was Ted Talbot's black and white photograph in Steam in Turkey *at this precise location that drew me to Eğridir on 11 September 1986, specifically to see and photograph the 18.00 departure with the lake as the backdrop. As he says in his caption, 'So Eğridir remains the terminus of a spectacular if sparsely served branch' — a reference to the fact that politics created this remote and unlikely railway terminus. The Ottoman Railway Company (ORC) intended to extend the line from here onwards to Konya before the First World War, but the Ottoman Government changed its previously-favoured plans, supporting instead the German-sponsored Baghdad Railway. Unlike Antalya, Eğridir is 'real Turkey'. In charge is 'Kriegslok' 2-10-0 No 56550.*

The evening sun highlights the smokebox of 'Kriegslok' 2-10-0 No 56550, waiting to depart with train No 1406, the 18.00 from Eğridir to Burdur. The foliage hides the fact that Eğridir station had been badly damaged by fire, but it is a remote and idyllic place, and this is the only departing train of the day, 11 September 1986.

The engine arrived — or was due to arrive, during the currency of the contemporary timetable — with train number 1401, which departs Burdur at 05.35 and is due in Eğridir at 08.55. It lies over for nine hours, simmering in the sun: not the most economical use of motive power, but illustrating the remoteness of this place.

the station, recently burned down, and at this remote outpost discovered a West German railwayman on the footplate of the engine simmering at the platform end. He had come to Eğridir to travel in the cab of the Standard 2-10-0 which stood quietly in dappled sunshine at the head of Train No 1406, the 18.00 departure to Burdur. It was an idyllic scene, redolent of the rural branch-line atmosphere of a Britain long ago. Everyone smiled. With the aid of interpretation amongst German, Swiss, British and Turkish members of the 'Brotherhood of Steam', we were promised good smoke over the bridge. We left the station, headed up the road, parked our car at the point where the road was nearest the bridge, and set forth on foot up the hillside and through the scrub for the bridge. I had been aware of another car parked near to ours, but gave it no thought as, with spring-heeled alacrity, I led my two colleagues under the bridge and further up the hillside, to gain a vantage point where the train, crossing the bridge, would have the azure background of Lake Eğridir.

Surely Scott's heartache at the knowledge of Amundsen could not have exceeded mine at that moment. Eğridir seemed far enough from civilization to guarantee solitude, but 'twas not to be. That car had brought both a photographer and a sound recordist to capture the sight and sound of steam storming the gradient from the lake-level station, up to and over the bridge, and on around the mountainside. My reward for the journey was a number of reasonable photographs, but sharing the view with another photographer was to diminish the satisfaction of the occasion, just as there is no real thrill in photographing special steam runs. Nevertheless, we had a good long day chasing steam, and Burdur Shed had been a sight, smell and sound from long ago. 'Twixt writing these words and checking my proofs, perhaps I have allowed my desire for 'photo-solitude' to dim my appreciation of Eğridir; it really is a delightful place. Turkish delight, indeed.

Earlier I 'trailered' the visit Jane and I made to Sivas Works Guest House. This was the first overnight stop on a four-day marathon we undertook with Canip and Ceyda Orhun to Turkey's 'Far East'. From Sivas we headed for Erzincan where we tracked down that elusive '8F'; thence to Erzurum, ostensibly the last main-line steam outpost on the way to the Russian border. With seven locomotives still active, Erzurum shed was the busiest steam depot on the main line, albeit not for long to judge by the information provided. However, 'information provided' in Turkey ranges through the inaccurate to the misleading — not always malicious, but sometimes so. Having been assured of a warm welcome at Sivas, as referred to earlier, we left Ankara with plans to accept the proffered hospitality of accommodation at the Sivas Railway Works Guest House. Well, that was my intention, Jane still hoping, perhaps, to find an hotel which might proffer something more akin to that to which she is accustomed. That we stayed at the Guest House should act as a warning to any fastidious spouse accompanying an adventurous railway-enthusiast husband to Eastern Turkey.... Wondering who had slept in the sheets and used one's towels merely added to the spice of uncertainty. Whatever may have been lacking in sophistication, elegance or refinement was, however, amply compensated for in hospitality. As our arrival was in mid to late afternoon, I was anxious to complete the formalities at the Guest House as quickly as good manners would permit. That done, Canip, Ceyda, Jane and I, accompanied by our hosts, made our way to the Works.

Even with permission to visit arranged through the Turkish Prime Minister's office, Jane and I were invited to surrender our passports before entering the Works Headquarters. The welcome, however, from Mr Ibrahim Yasan, and from the Depot Manager Mr Orhan Yildirim, was warm, firm and categorical. Ere long we were off around the works, having been told unequivocally that the repair of steam locomotives at Sivas had totally finished and that the only steam engines I would see were in long rows — rank upon rank of dead engines. The atmosphere inside the works, now filled only with diesel locomotives, was for me both wistful and melancholy. Jane was forced to nudge me hard to take some interest in what was being told and shown to us, but my aim was to get outside; a dead steam-engine was of infinitely more interest than the sight of diesels under repair.

Mindful of my earlier assurance that this chapter is not to become an extended version of 'The Adleys' Travels in Turkey', let me stick to the steam-related facts. As my three travelling-companions were whisked away on a tour of Sivas, I 'escaped' from the diesel-dripping works into the fading afternoon sun. Heading for the shed, the lines of withdrawn and dumped steam-engines soon hove into view. Accompanied by a posse of staff, my camera was soon in action. Numbers were scribbled into my notepad. As usual, I took inadequate care to procure as much detailed information as might have been available within the limitations of the language barrier. Manufacturers' workplates provided much information, and I knew that Ted Talbot's bible of Turkish steam would enable me to classify and accurately to annotate the subjects at which my camera was aimed: 'Kriegslok 2-10-0'; 'Baldwin 2-8-2'; 'Nohab 2-8-0'; 'Czech 2-10-0'; 'Turkish-built 2-10-0'; 'VIW 2-10-0'; 'Stretched Prussian P8 4-8-0'; 'Lima 2-8-2'; there was no shortage of variety.

Ugly, carbuncular manifestation of American steam: Vulcan Iron Works (Wilkes Barre, not Newton-le-Willows) 2-10-0 No 56362, built in 1949, rusts away amongst endless lines of dumped TCDD locomotives at Sivas on 17 September 1986. Nobody steals number-plates, but the headlamp, which sat on the ledge at the top of the smokebox door, has long gone.

Lack of detailed knowledge plus unfamiliarity reduces but by no means eliminates interest in rusting hulks in foreign lands. As the end of steam in Britain approaches its twentieth anniversary, more and more intrepid travellers scour the world for hidden caches of dead steam. Sometimes, as in Bangkok in late 1986, I come across unexpected gems such as a 1910 Brush-built 0-6-0T. It was with immeasurable satisfaction therefore that amongst the German, Swedish, Czechoslovakian and American hulks at Sivas, the unmistakable shape of a Stanier '8F' presented itself to me. Believing there still to be one, and only one, of the twenty 'Churchills' — as they are known in Turkey — still in steam, it was clearly not going to be at Sivas. Thus, suddenly coming across an '8F' amongst the lines of foreigners brought me a thrill and excitement that was clearly incomprehensible to my hosts. The sun was fading; she was not only rusting but had clearly been involved in an accident. But an '8F' is an '8F'.

Having paid homage to this 'unknown warrior', I headed along the tracks beside Sivas' old steam sheds, and there were two more of Stanier's masterpieces. One was in fact impossible to identify, but TCDD No 45170 (NBL Works No 24755:1942:WD554) was clearly recognisable. As the sun and the horizon sought to come to their inevitable tryst I waited; would the shadow of a nondescript hut obscure the rays of the setting sun's attempt to illuminate the smokebox of my fellow-countryman? My pleasure was thrice-rewarded when another 8F, No 45166 (NBL Works No 24641:1941:WD341) yielded itself to my hungry eyes; an unforgettable sunset sight.

Dinner at Sivas Railway Guest House was a family affair. There would be more to see in the morning. Turkish television was not much of an incentive to keep us from our bed, Jane already beginning to regret that our 'holiday' was ending, rather than commencing, with our steam-search. Her emotions were hardly soothed when the mournful works siren awakened us; at 5.50 the next morning my feelings of nostalgia for such an audible reminder of the industrial revolution were quite definitely not shared by my long-suffering spouse. My determination to return to the 'old' and 'new' steam sheds put a further strain on marital bliss, which at Sivas is better contemplated now in recollection than 'enjoyed' at the time of its occurence. Nevertheless, we partook of an excellent breakfast and the home-made butter and yoghurt were delicious. Having been assured that steam was dead and buried at Sivas, my feelings may only be imagined at the sight of smoke drifting into the bright, still morning air. This was 18 September 1986, and there, alive, well and active, was a 2-10-0, shunting. Only by selfish insistence on returning there before our departure had I been able, yet again, to confound the 'information' given to me the previous day. Not wishing to query with my hosts the inaccuracy of their words of yesterday, I used my time to the utmost with my camera. No 56156 was a Skoda-built (in 1949) Standard 2-10-0. First supplied by Henschel

Sivas Works has now finished with steam, and the vast acreage contains various dumps of engines, some long-condemned to the scrap lines. Wistfully, I wandered amongst unfamiliar hulks. The sight that suddenly confronted me took my breath away: as the blood-red setting sun confronted the rust and tangled with the lengthening shadows, I waited until the last possible moment to capture this shot of what my guide — who knew not of Stanier — called a 'Churchill' (see page 138). Built in 1941 by the North British Locomotive Company Ltd, Glasgow, TCDD No 45166 is an '8F' 2-8-0 in a far corner of a foreign field, faded, forlorn and forgotten — but my heart overflowed. 17 September 1986.

in 1937, orders were placed for more of the class with Vulcan Foundry, Robert Stephenson and Beyer Peacock, some of which engines as well as other European manufacturers, were amongst those dumped at Sivas. The final batch of engines, Nos 56142-66 were ordered from Skoda, and it was one of these that was at work.

On leaving 56156 to her duties, I returned with my guide/companion to the Depot Manager's office. Having asked Orhan Yildirim about the role of the living 2-10-0 he said 'it is not an engine working as a locomotive, but acting as a mobile boiler'. Perhaps my terminology would need to be changed for future questioning, although to be fair the duties being fulfilled by 56156 bore little resemblance to shunting in Whitemoor Yards... It would be unfair to have remonstrated about information provided, especially as he took immense trouble to obtain for me detailed information about the steam engines still allocated to five depots in 'Division 4', namely Erzincan, Erzurum, Divriği, Çetinkaya and Samsun.

It was during my sojourn at Sivas that I solved the terminological problems emanating from TCDD's designation of Stanier '8F's as 'Churchills'. Originally twenty-five of these fine engines were shipped to Turkey by the War Department. The tale of their despatch is neatly encapsulated by Ted Talbot:

'Thus in the early 1940s, Turkey found itself extremely short of power. There were only some 500 locomotives on the standard gauge throughout the whole country, most of them small and many of them old (present-day visitors to the Zonguldak line may well wonder how the engines then available coped with its gradients). The problem seems to have been solved politically, by playing off one side against the other. Both the British and the Germans were anxious to win favour with the neutral Turks. The British ambassador in Ankara discovered, or was allowed to discover, that the Germans were to supply the Turks with locomotives, and made an urgent appeal to London for British locomotives to be supplied also. There was already concern at the War Office about the capacity of the railways in Turkey, if it were necessary for British troops to enter the country to counter a German invasion, and the result was that Stanier '8F's being built by North British for the War Department were delivered to the TCDD. Eventually the British, Germans and Americans all supplied their "war" locomotives to neutral Turkey!'

Different angles, changing light: the following morning the '8F' seems almost ready for coal, water and crew: alas, 'tis not to be, as she awaits her fate on the scrap road at Sivas, on 18 September 1986.

This, according to my hosts, is not a 'working steam engine', merely a 'mobile heating boiler' — I suppose it is possible to differentiate between such terminological exactitudes. However, Skoda Standard 2-10-0 No 56156 was alive, well, working and on the move at Sivas early in the morning of 18 September 1986. North-south tracks, at right angles to the low sun, hide the smokebox — but, just behind the Skoda's tender, the sun highlights the sad, battered boiler of Stanier '8F' ('Churchill') 2-8-0, TCDD No 45170, the last of the batch supplied to Turkey, built in 1942. She is dwarfed by another dead locomotive, face to face.

'Churchills' they were called, and that they have remained. My pleasure at finding three of the dead engines still at Sivas was but an hors-d'oeuvre to the anticipation of hoping to find one in steam. The information gleaned from various sources before leaving home pointed to the slight possibility of one being active still at Erzincan. On the list compiled for me at Sivas by Orhan Yildirim, three '8F's — numbers 45156/62/63 — were still officially allocated to Erzincan shed. It seemed highly unlikely. Before leaving Sivas that morning I had a last look at 45166, persuading an itinerant and his donkey to pose alongside the engine. From the floor of the cab I stole an injector handle, for return to the land of its birth. We returned to the Railway Guest House, expressed our gratitude and bade Sivas farewell.

Only those unfamiliar with Erzincan could have approached the town with such keen anticipation. Harvesting was nearing completion; the September sun was still hot at midday. The mountains of the Anatolian high plateau stretched as far ahead and around as the eye could see. Reasonably happy in the knowledge that our TCDD friends at Sivas had phoned through to Erzincan shed to announce our impending arrival, I succumbed to the desire, on the part of Canip, Ceyda and Jane, for lunch. An ordinary meal in a boring and not very clean hotel in a town that looked more Bulgarian than Turkish did not encourage any longing to linger. We left the hotel, went to the station, obtained directions to the shed, and headed away from the town centre.

Erzincan is not a large town. It sits astride the main road about three-fifths of the way between Sivas and Erzerum. Not surprisingly it featured in none of the guides to Turkey with which we had equipped ourselves. In spite of all this, my sense of anticipation ran high as we left the built-up area behind. The 'built-up area' comprised little more than two main streets crossing in the centre of the town. The buildings were squat, featureless and modern in a 1950s style, soon giving way to dusty roadsides. The mountains looked much more attractive than the town we left behind. The dirt-track which we sought was self-evidently leading to a building standing alone, adjacent to the railway tracks. A plume of black smoke wandered lazily upwards from an unseen locomotive hidden from view by the shed building as we approached. It was about 2 o'clock in the afternoon, hot and dusty as we drew up alongside the depot. By this time my anticipation had reached fever pitch, but the sight of a dead '8F' brought a bitter taste to my mouth as Canip sought Mustafa Gakici, the depot manager. I checked my cameras. Canip returned; permission was granted. Stumbling, running now, towards that plume of black smoke, my quest to see that last of the 'Churchills' in steam was about to be satisfied or dashed.

Jane was keeping up with me; simultaneously we stopped in our tracks. An '8F'. In steam. Here, now, at Erzincan, Turkey, 18 September 1986. The last of the 'Churchills', TCDD No 45156, built by the North British Locomotive Company in 1941, works number 24646, War Department No 346. Quite simply, the locomotive at which we were looking was the last ordinary working Stanier '8F' 2-8-0 in normal use on any railway in the world. It was quite unmistakable, only the Westinghouse brake, chimney cap and the small cow-catcher setting the engine visually apart from its hundreds of sister engines, most of which, between 1935 and 1968, served the railways of Britain with consummate efficiency.

Rupert Brooke's words rang in my ears, this corner of a foreign field reminding me in a number of ways of Carnforth. Erzincan's place on the map is as much to do with its railway geography as anything else. The shed stands more in rural than in urban surroundings. Whilst the bare Anatolian mountains are more dramatic — and as a distant backdrop more photogenic — than the hills of Furness and the Lake District, there was a similar atmosphere at Erzincan 1986 to Carnforth 1968; lines of dead engines awaiting scrapping, an air of change, and of course an '8F' in steam. Unfortunately there is no evidence of the emergence of a Turkish Bill McAlpine to set up an Anatolian Steamtown; merely to write such fanciful words highlights the fundamental and total difference between the real world of Erzincan and the reality of railway preservation with its gleaming engines and 'family appeal'.

I could have spent many hours at that shed, but although Canip

Overleaf *Quite simply the last Stanier '8F' 2-8-0 in steam on a national railway system anywhere in the world. I had travelled far, and in hope, to Erzincan in eastern Turkey. My reward was great: TCDD number 45156 shunting in the shed yard on 18 September 1986. In the right background, dead, sister '8F' No 45163 faces the shed, dominated by the surrounding Anatolian mountains.*

Phoney photographic poses were unnecessary: albeit cluttered by alien paraphernalia, Stanier's classic lines proclaim themselves.

Orhun as our 'host, friend and guide' never showed an iota of impatience, neither of our wives relished the thought of driving in the dark from Erzincan to Erzurum. My ambition to see the lowering sun on the flanks of 45156 conflicted with the understandable desire of the rest of the party to head east. The road from Erzincan to Erzurum would be a tortuous journey through endless mountain ranges. Before we left, however, I had located two more '8Fs' TCDD Nos 45162 and 45163 had long since dropped their last fires, but their unmistakable shape nevertheless brought a lump to my throat. The scores of photographs taken will last, hopefully, as long as need be... We could not reach Erzurum before dark; those Turkish trucks are aimed not driven, and night driving in Turkey is definitely not recommended.

It would be simple to write extensively not only of Erzincan but even more so of Erzurum, itself the main target now for the balding British railway enthusiasts for whom Armageddon arrived with the end of British steam in August 1968. Already this chapter is too long; each word is as a piston-stroke in motion approaching the buffers represented by my publisher's requirements. A clean and agreeable hotel in Erzurum helped to maintain the equilibrium insofar as the patience and tolerance of our little party was concerned. I knew that the following day would probably be my last chance extensively to photograph steam at work in Turkey; and so it proved.

As early as reasonably possible the next morning, Canip and I left the Oral hotel. Perhaps it should be emphasized again that eastern Turkey does not exactly welcome railway enthusiasts. Hardly anyone speaks English and, as I was to discover before that day was out, apprehension by the railway authorities, the military and/or the secret police is inevitable. With Canip's help and company, however, the day started well. Ujeyir Ülker, the young and enthusiastic depot manager at Erzurum Shed, gave us a most friendly welcome. The inevitable and enjoyable tea provided an opportunity to swap reminiscences. He proudly showed me a postcard of *Mallard* in that ghastly blue livery, whilst I proffered some shots of Erzurum Station, a 2-10-0 and its crew taken a few months earlier by a participant in one of those intrepid package tours of Eastern Turkey organized by Gail Jopling, wife of the former Minister of Agriculture. The photographs were taken by Michael Wade; handing them to the shedmaster caused him to guffaw, and ring his office bell. Minutes later one of the crew in the photograph appeared in the office; more bonhomie and joviality all round.

Having completed a preliminary and somewhat cursory inspection of the shed, I was able to photograph train number 1930, the 09.10 departure from Erzurum to Horasan, hauled by Skoda Standard 2-10-0 No 56162. More photography on the main line adjacent to the shed, with the station in the background, was a pleasurable reminder of a still mainly steam railway scene. CKD Standard 2-10-0 took water,

obligingly. The local trains from Erzurum to Horasan to the east, and to Karasu to the west, were still steam-hauled, albeit two-coach trains with excessive 2-10-0 motive power, a sure sign that they were in their steam swansong. They were in the twilight 'twixt elimination of elderly locomotives more suited to the strength of the task in hand, and the total elimination of steam when appropriate diesel motive power arrives out here in the Turkish 'far east'.

On our return to Ujeyir Ülker's office, he agreed to let me wander around his shed at leisure. As I inspected some of the more interesting engines on the scrap-line, including Nohab 0-6-0T No 3322, I was aware that I was, as they say, not alone. Mistakenly assuming that my 'companion' was merely expressing a railwayman's friendly interest in my activities, I kept clicking away. His demeanour very soon changed from inquisitiveness to menace; shouting and waving his arms at me, he strode in my direction, yelling by now in Turkish to which I was unable to respond. As he lunged for my camera, I made off very fast indeed back into the shed, hotly pursued right into the depot manager's office where, fortunately, Ujeyir Ülker and Canip were still busy chatting. Thus was I saved from the first of three interceptions that day.

It is necessary here briefly to refer to NATO's eastern flank, its con-

No doubting the place from which Skoda Standard 2-10-0 No 56162 departs with train No 1930, the 09.10 from Erzurum to Horasan, on 19 September 1986. The smoke effects were certainly not cosmetically ordered for the camera — and I wonder what the chap on the platform was trying to achieve?

In the brief period between the taking of this photograph, and its appearance in the book, the retreat of steam has continued apace. In Steam Railway, November 1987, David Thornhill reports: 'Mid-June saw all line work out of Erzurum dieselized, both the suburban trains and the Kars mixed. The final steam loco on the latter duty was 56121 on June 11'. So yet another sight is sadly relegated from the 'current' file, to 'memories'.

Erzurum station pilot, Standard 2-10-0 No 56141, takes water between duties on 19 September 1986. This engine was the final one of twenty-five built for TCDD by Českomoravská-Kolben-Danek A Sp, Prague (CKD), in 1949.

My visit, that day, to Erzurum shed, left me indubitably with the feeling that I should never see a working steam depot here again. Sadly, that foreboding was accurate.

tiguity with the Russian border and the history of Turkish-Soviet relations, to appreciate the very visible and active level of security in this area. Canip and I, having left the shed and returned to the hotel, collected our wives and set off out of Erzurum towards Kars. Our intention was to combine some rural and archaeological sightseeing with the possibility of photographing steam in the countryside. Our intended destination was Hasankale, where a magnificent fortress overlooks the town and the railway line. We hoped to be there in time to catch sight of train number 1931, the 11.43 from Horasan to Erzurum, due to stop at Hasankale at 12.59. Our initial objective was not facilitated by arrival at a place called Pasinler, which appeared to be where Hasankale should have been! However, after consulting various maps, it appeared to be the right place, known by either name; such is life in Turkey.

Having found a good location for my photograph, we waited, and waited. By now surrounded by inquisitive youngsters, we were advised that anticipating the arrival of the train at the hour designated in the timetable was considered to be an act of extreme optimism, not to say stupidity. We left our spot, wandered round the small town, bought some local bread rolls, found another pitch by the track in the town, and finally were rewarded with the sight of 56162 returning at the head of the train for which we had waited. It seems that the 'timetable' had been amended, so we were told later, for departure ex Horasan at 12.15, not 11.43, but this was somewhat academic.

With Canip again at the wheel of our elderly air-conditioned Mercedes, we headed out of Hasankale — or Pasinler, as you prefer — our intention being to overhaul the train and photograph it out in the open spaces 'twixt there and Erzurum. We found a place beside the main road giving extensive views up a gorge where the gradient against the train promised some good smoke-effects, notwithstanding the sun being somewhat less than perfectly positioned. In sight of the distant tank and gun-emplacements on the hillsides, I set up my tripod.

The 'secret police' arrived within minutes. Happily, they appeared forewarned of our presence in the area and, having ascertained my identity, left us in peace. Again I was indebted to Canip as, naturally, English was not spoken. TCDD is almost entirely a single-track railway system apart from the immediate vicinity of the largest stations, thus we had to await the passing eastbound of a diesel-hauled freight before, at last, 56162 rounded the bend at the bottom of the gorge. With the regulator open-as she pounded up the grade, we were well rewarded; then, to the relief of Ceyda and Jane, we set off back to Erzurum. Notwithstanding reports to the contrary, the diesels had already arrived on some of the trains 'twixt Erzurum and Kars. Erzurum, the only settlement in Anatolia located 1,950 metres above sea level, is totally different from Erzincan, as interesting as the latter is boring. The Silk Road passed through the city, which contains many interesting old buildings. Whilst the girls had done their sightseeing in the morning when Canip and I were at the engine-shed, Ceyda, an inveterate shopper, joined me in a shopping/sightseeing tour. Wandering through the old quarter, I was unable to resist the temptation to sample the interior of the local Turkish Bath. Ceyda went on her way, leaving me to enjoy an experience that is not exactly on the tourist trail! A bath, massage, local tea, and the use of towels, slippers, etc set me back the princely sum of 50 pence: I emerged, refreshed, glowing additionally in the knowledge that I had provided some amusement for the Turkish Bath's local clients, who appeared not to be used to the presence of foreigners, let alone ones who spoke not a word of the language. My reinvigoration, however, spurred me on to one final visit, on my own, to Erzurum Station, to try to photograph the evening departures of the steam-hauled 'locals' to Horasan and Karasu.

This time I was really thoroughly apprehended, by a full platoon of the Turkish Army led by a very brisk officer. Totally alone, without any prior notice having been given nor permission sought, my position was tricky. Happily, I had a copy on me of the 'To Whom It May Concern' letter from the Turkish Ambassador in London, Rahmi Gumrukcuoglu, to which reference was made earlier. I produced it, handed it to the officer, and tried to look nonchalant. He read it carefully — and addressed me in French. Fortunately he had been with NATO in Paris. Ever thankful to my French master at Uppingham, we managed to converse. My House of Commons identity card helped and soon we were discussing the merits of 'chemin de fer vapeur' — at least, that is what I was endeavouring to articulate. The platoon were stood down and shortly, with protestations of goodwill, they withdrew.

Standard 2-10-0 No 56169 departed at 17.40 with the train for Karasu, unfortunately tender-first as the sun was, this time, splendid. The big engine glided effortlessly out of the station with its diminutive two-coach load. At the other end of the station another 2-10-0 — my familiar friend No 56162 — waited at the head of train number 1930, the 18.15 'mixed' to Horasan. It was the end of a magnificent autumn day. The sun, fast diving behind the distant mountains, was not prepared to wait. As 56162 blew off, the chill of the evening became noticeable. Erzurum has an inhospitable climate; hot and dry summers quickly change to cold and severe winters of long duration. The sun had already dipped below the hills as 56162 pulled out, heading east. Vainly I took some shots of her. By now it was getting cold. Winter was near; so too, I felt, was the end of steam on the main line, although nothing is certain in Turkey. Wistfully I watched the big engine glide away into the distance. I knew in my bones that that was to be my last photograph of steam at Erzurum...It had been a memorable day.

That night in Erzurum we dined well on a local speciality of charcoal-grilled baby trout. This place may not be a renowned gastronomic centre, but it had provided me with full reward for a long journey. The following morning we began the journey back, eventually to Ankara. It would have been too far to do the journey comfortably in one day, even had we planned so to do. Our overnight sojourn was to be Amasya, turning north from the main highway at Refahiye. The road map was as reliable as the *Yolcu Rehberi*, TCDD's timetable. Metalled road gave way to what is euphemistically described as 'stone road'. Suddenly, rounding a bend, we were confronted literally with a wall of earth. Two huge machines had placed boulders as big as trucks across the 'road'. For an hour we were ambushed. It was late afternoon before we arrived at Amasya and I knew that Jane's enthusiasm for this adventure had evaporated. As she sank, exhausted, on to the bed, Canip accompanied me on one final sortie; Amasya was on the line from Sivas to Samsun, where steam allegedly still survived. Amasya station was deserted; we eventually found a railwayman who said that no steam-hauled trains ran any more on this long line from Sivas to the Black Sea. The wind whistled through the once-elegant station buildings; autumn leaves swirled. We were not going to Samsun. I had seen the last of steam on this trip. Tomorrow we should be back in Ankara, thence to Istanbul, and home. As I write these words, it is only six months ago — it seems an era, a lifetime.

LAST
STRONGHOLD
OF STEAM

'Rain stopped play' is inappropriate, inaccurate and unfair insofar as it relates to my railway photography in and around England's northern capital. As with all my activity, it was very much a case of 'too little, too late' to be able accurately to represent the vivid variety of railway operations that inevitably characterized such an important industrial and commercial centre.

As with other cities, the construction of the railways from the early Victorian years had a profound effect on the social fabric of Manchester and indeed of the suburban and outer suburban areas into Cheshire and Lancashire. From the opening of the first railway in 1830, the population grew steadily; indeed, if one includes Salford — as any non-Mancunian is likely to do — the population growth up to the period of the First World War was considerably faster than in that other Lancastrian city at the other end of the Liverpool & Manchester Railway. Indeed, this pioneer line originally terminated at Salford, so giving me my excuse or reason fairly widely to encompass the area of 'Manchester' for the purposes of this chapter.

As with the other great railway cities, great changes have occurred in the railway map of Manchester, and once famous railway termini have been relegated from passenger to goods stations. By 1842, the city already boasted five main lines that radiated from four terminal stations, each situated close to the edge of the central built-up area. The Liverpool & Manchester railway had arrived at Liverpool Road Station in 1830, and another line, to Bolton, was built from Salford in 1836. By 1840 the railway had arrived from Leeds, terminating at Oldham Road Station. Finally, in 1842 the lines from Sheffield and from Birmingham had 'set up shop' in what was then known as Store Street Station.

Although technically there was an element of competition for the Manchester-Birmingham traffic between the Manchester & Birmingham from Store Street and the Liverpool & Manchester/Grand Junction route via Warrington and Crewe, those early years saw the establishment of basic positions into Manchester, by non-competing railways from different directions. A new line to Macclesfield, linking with the North Staffordshire Railway through the Potteries, opened

In Victoria's terminus section, the station pilot on 5 June 1968, Newton Heath's 'Black Five' 4-6-0 No 45076, stands in the centre road, steam gently escaping. An oily rag has been applied to her smokebox, but the diesel multiple unit in the background is the evil harbinger of a steam-extinct future two months hence: and this very engine was withdrawn a few days later.

The sight, smell and sound of a stationary locomotive under the roof of a major railway station, epitomized the very feeling of the steam era — steam to spare, controlled power, man's created workhorse, primeval harnessing of the elements — the removal of which from our lives left an unfillable gap.

in 1849. Nevertheless, the initial rail development of and in Manchester saw the city as a hub, with railway lines radiating therefrom as spokes.

Anyone cocooned in a time machine awakening today and seeking to catch a train from 'Liverpool Road', 'Oldham Road' or even 'Store Street' stations would be in a fix. The changes wrought by the need to cater for through traffic soon turned Liverpool Road and Oldham Road into goods termini. It was in 1844 that Manchester Victoria opened to replace these two stations as well as Salford, itself translated to goods use (see the map on page 163). The main feature of this new line, involving major urban engineering, was the viaduct up to the junction of the Leeds lines at Miles Platting. To the end of steam, the 1 in 47 gradient of Miles Platting Bank eastbound out of Victoria Station was a hurdle which necessitated the permanent stationing of banking engines at Victoria. Locomotives charging the bank were an unforgettable sight.

To the south of the city centre, outside and not directly accessible to Store Street Station, was built a link which gave trains from the Sheffield and Birmingham companies a direct link with the Liverpool line. This line's inaccessibility to Store Street terminus for eastbound trains actually perpetuated that station's terminal status. However, in

keeping with the public relations activities at which the railway companies became so adept, the name 'Store Street' was changed to 'London Road', which stood the test of time until recent years when the station was renamed Manchester Piccadilly. Station name changes could themselves merit a sociological study. The Store Street/London Road/Piccadilly syndrome well illustrates the fashions of the era — from 'strictly locationally factual' to 'railway promotional' to 'geographically socially desirable'. Mancunians, or at least railway enthusiasts thereabouts, will hopefully understand what I am talking about.

What am I talking about? With my pencil taking charge, and urging itself on across inviting blank paper, there is a danger that this chapter may give itself airs and graces and seek to become a potted history of railway development in Manchester. There is no possibility that my very limited knowledge could remotely equip me for such a task. There are numerous learned tomes ably accomplishing what is, by any standards, a very complex undertaking; and there are, frankly and sadly, a few failed attempts too. The truthful answer then to my soliloquized enquiry as to the object of this chapter is to match some of my photographs taken in steam's last stronghold with some related

Those familiar with the daily activity at Manchester Victoria in steam days will recognize this location — the waiting position for the engines standing by to assist eastbound trains up Miles Platting Bank. Newton Heath's 'Black Five' 4-6-0 No 44780 is on duty on 24 June 1968, a few days before inevitable withdrawal: this may be her last day of active duty.

Eastbound trains faced a fearsome tussle out of Victoria, with Miles Platting Bank offering 1,200 yards at 1 in 59, 720 yards at 1 in 47 and 425 yards at 1 in 178. Westbound goods trains, both from Newton Heath and Ashton Moss, were required to stop and pin down brakes before descending.

Previous page *Colour photographs of steam at Manchester Central are rare. Now closed, and with part of the site encompassed within a conference centre, this 'period piece' picture was taken from the window of the departing 12.25 train to St Pancras. Stanier '4MT' 2-6-4T No 42465 of 8F Springs Branch, Wigan, in her last year of active life, blows off impatiently at the head of a local train on 1 April 1964. The station closed on 5 May 1969.*

The superb arched glass roof comprised a single span of 210 ft, rising to a height of 90 ft above rail level. Although the station — or that part of it covered by the magnificent roof — contained only six platforms, each contained a centre track between those alongside the platforms. The lines on the left of this picture, outside the roof, ran to the former CLC goods station.

comments about the city around which this steam activity radiated. Inevitably one bumps immediately into the need to define one's geographical limits, and I need to avoid falling foul of the earlier chapter entitled '10A, 10D, 10F', known to the *cognoscenti* as the shed codes of Carnforth, Lostock Hall and Rose Grove respectively. Let me decide herewith that the geographical delineation of the chapter shall be that area encompassed and served by the motive power depots of DO9 — Manchester Division, London Midland Region, British Railways, as at the end of the steam era. Now we can return to Manchester itself.

Counting Exchange and Victoria as one, and adding London Road and Central, the city centre hosted three great passenger railway stations at the end of the steam era, none of which was linked directly; however, after more than 150 years, central Government approval and authorization has at least been given to link the Bolton line with the main line to the South. This new line, the Windsor Link, will doubtless transform the role and position of Manchester insofar as its rail services are concerned; but that is for the future and this book is concerned inexorably with the past.

Manchester's third city centre station, like London Road but unlike Victoria/Exchange a terminus, was Central, completed in 1880 and the site of my first railway photograph in the city in March 1963. It was the home of the Cheshire Lines Committee (CLC). Owned jointly by the Great Central, Great Northern and Midland Railways, it provided one of the three main lines eventually linking Manchester with Liverpool, the others being the Lancashire & Yorkshire (L & Y) and the London and North Western (LNW) Railways. Manchester Central, with its part-Midland, part-Great Central parentage, was not unlike St Pancras or Marylebone — in numbers of platforms fairly small, but in architectural splendour mighty. That first visit yielded the sole example of an LNER locomotive that DO9 ever presented to my camera; a late-night, murky photograph of 'B1' 4-6-0 No 61369 awaiting departure with the 23.05 Manchester Central to Marylebone 'express'. The inverted commas are intended to be derogatory, for by this date the Great Central Railway was as a plump swimmer confronting a hungry shark — BR management had sealed its fate. The occasion of the visit is to me more memorable than the outcome of my camera work, not least because my trusty Voigtlander Vito CLR was loaded with the dreaded Gevacolour.

That murky March night gave me the flavour of Manchester, and my mind was to be tested in the coming years to creating opportunities to visit the area. As a young, recently-married businessman based in London, with no immediately obvious reason to spend much of my employer's time and money in the north-west, it took some ingenuity for me to create the varied 'reasons'. However, from April Fools Day the following year until the end of steam in August 1968, my visits multiplied: but they were by no means to my entire satisfaction, with neither remotely sufficient time, nor with adequate planning or intelligence. Perhaps it is worth documenting these forays, bearing in mind that they had to be fitted into the timetable of a reasonably conscientious worker whose family commitments prevented weekend visits, certainly until political activity saw me adopted as prospective Parliamentary candidate for Birkenhead in 1965. By then, of course, Birkenhead and indeed Merseyside was a frequent weekend haunt, but outside the scope of this chapter, devoted as it is to DO9:

Mar 63	Manchester Central
31 Mar 64	New Mills
1 April 64	Manchester Central; Cheadle Heath; Peak Forest
22 April 64	Clifton Junction
23 April 64	Plumley
June 64	Clifton Junction
1 Dec 64	Patricroft
Dec 64	Newton Heath
5 Mar 65	Patricroft
Jan 66	Oldham
9 Mar 67	Stockport
10 Mar 67	Manchester Piccadilly; Stockport
25 July 67	Manchester Victoria/Exchange; Ordsall Lane
10 Aug 67	Manchester Victoria/Exchange; Stockport
21 Dec 67	Trafford Park
4 June 68	Haslingden and Helmshore
5 June 68	Manchester Victoria
24 June 68	Stockport; Manchester Victoria/Exchange; Bolton
25 June 68	Bolton
Aug 68	Bolton

The mere act of extracting and recording this information illustrates both the 'Mancunian Gap' created by my politically-necessitated activity in Birkenhead leading up to the 1966 general election and the fact that the final few weeks of steam in July and early August 1968 were concentrated on those last three sheds referred to earlier. Nevertheless, Manchester can certainly claim, as Britain's cities were electrified and dieselized, to be the last stronghold of steam; befitting indeed to the place which can justifiably claim to be both England's Northern capital and the commercial cradle of the (steam-driven) industrial revolution.

Between 1801 and 1901 the population of Manchester rose from 70,000 to 544,000. Whilst geography had ensured the city's importance since Roman times, to the natural and visible features of the preindustrial era could be added the proximity of coal together with the attributes of humidity and soft water so essential to the textile industry. Immediately prior to the dawn of the railway era, canals had already put Manchester at the web of transport links to Bury, Bolton and Rochdale to the north and north-west; to Ashton and through to Yorkshire; south to the Midlands; and to Runcorn, the Mersey and the sea via the Duke of Bridgewater's canal. (It is a source of irritation to me to see either this 'Bridgewater' or the Somerset 'Bridgwater' misspelt — just a personal quirk.)

As steam-powered factories transformed Manchester, so the railways sought to establish themselves. Sadly for Manchester, less enthusiasm was initially shown hereabouts than was manifested by its Lancastrian rival metropolis at the mouth of the Mersey. The determination in those early years to keep the railways out of the city centre blighted the vision of those who saw the city as the natural staging-post 'twixt north and south of the country. Indeed, for 150 years passengers have regretted that early hostility to which I referred earlier in this chapter, and which has led fascinated railway authors and historians eternally to write articles such as 'Manchester — The Divided City' by Martin Bairstow in the *Railway Magazine* for October 1986. In a brief debate on the railways in the House of Commons that same month, I was able to refer to the historic significance of the Windsor link.

There is no better guide-book to this day than Churton's *The Rail Road Book of England* from which to glean the significance of the railway in assessing the growth and status of our cities and towns. 'Manchester' first appears on page 46 in the first main chapter, entitled 'London To Edinburgh via Birmingham'. After Wigan, 204½ miles from Euston, we note the 'Manchester-Southport Branch'. Thence, via the index, we finally reach the full reference to Manchester on page 380, as the terminating point of the line noted as 'Colwick to Manchester'. Churton describes Manchester as 'a place of great antiquity, and is supposed to be built upon the site of the Roman station Mancunium, which spot had previously been occupied by the Britons'. There follow details of the civic, artistic and architectural features of the city. The munificent description ends thus: 'The wonderful improvements in machinery, and the public spirit and industry of its inhabitants, have combined to render it the focus of the cotton manufacturers, of which it monopolises two-thirds of all that is produced in the empire. There are 186 cotton and silk mills and factories, employing 34,449 hands, and the force used is nearly equal to 10,000 horse power'.

Whilst these words ring splendidly of the material benefits of the industrial revolution, there is no mention of the squalor and hardship which was the inevitable by-product of the early years of industrialization. Nevertheless, such confidence and pride seems a far cry today from the timidity and self-denigration that seem so often to exemplify many of the towns and cities in which the industrial

revolution was forged. Where are the entrepreneurs, the innovators, the men of vision and energy whose names fill the pages of Churton?

Which of the photographic locations listed above shall we select for scrutiny? In an earlier book I wrote a chapter entitled 'The Battle of Clifton Junction'. Patricroft has also featured in an earlier tome. Here, the Liverpool & Manchester (L & M), the first railway into the city, crossed the Bridgewater Canal, encouraging the construction at this unimportant village, of the Bridgewater Foundry by Nasmyth Gaskill and Company in 1836. In 1850 a branch line was opened half a mile east of Patricroft from Eccles Junction to Springs Branch near Wigan (see the map on page 64). With the coming of the railway, residential districts of some prosperity sprung up hereabouts.

My visits to this area in 1964/5 pre-dated my deepening interest in railway history. Clifton Junction Station, and the signal boxes at the station and at Pepper Hill nearby, provided me with my first taste of the flavour of the railway in that area. My souvenirs are not entirely restricted to photography, for the Pepper Hill signalman kindly donated his hand-written record book of train movements which is, I suppose, of no interest or value to anyone but a dedicated enthusiast. In September 1986, Pepper Hill box, like so much of Manchester's railway heritage, was demolished. Opposite the box was, and still is, the tile

My vantage point for many photographs: Pepper Hill box, photographed in August 1980 and reduced to rubble in September 1986. Happily I have 'preserved' some of the signalmen's train records. That bridge has served me well photographically, too — it is featured on pages 156 and 157. How stylish and sturdy were the railway buildings of our forebears — and how dismal are today's flat-roofed shacks.

On a glorious evening, 22 April 1964, 'WD' 2-8-0 No 90592, of 10H Lower Darwen, drifts down the grade past Pepper Hill box near Clifton Junction with a Blackburn to Ancoats freight. Barely visible in the distance on the far right is Molyneux Viaduct on the now-closed line to Bury. Motorways sear the area hereabouts today, destroying scale, harmony and heritage.

No 90592 was but a few weeks away from withdrawal. Built in December 1943 as WD No 77147, loaned to the LNER in June 1947 and taken into BR stock on nationalization, she was withdrawn in June 1964 and scrapped at the Central Wagon Company, Ince, three months later.

factory of Messrs Pilkington. That my long-suffering colleagues in Commonwealth Holiday Inns of Canada (CHIC) still recognize the value of calendar tiles as a valuable marketing item is a direct link with the days when, as Sales Director of the May Fair Hotel, I ordered my first calendar tiles, using the visit to the Pilkington factory as the perfect reason — or excuse as some might suggest — for visits to the factory at about 3.30 pm. Thus was I enabled to silence my conscience about ending my working day around 4.15 and taking myself and my Voigtlander to the adjacent station and signal boxes to record the flow of steam-hauled commuter trains proceeding briskly westwards from Manchester Victoria. Happy times and happy days they were, too.

Clifton is a junction no more. The line from Clifton Junction northwards to Ringley Road and on to Bury has gone, and with it the track across elegant Molyneux Viaduct, of fond memory. My ignorance prevented me from exploring the remains of that nearby line from Patricroft to Molyneux Junction via Clifton Hall tunnel. Within three months of its opening in 1850, passenger traffic was withdrawn. With the exception of occasional excursion traffic before the Second World War when trains from the Lancashire cotton towns to the North Wales coast traversed the line through the tunnel, it rated little or no attention. Its main claim to fame came in April 1953 when part of the tunnel collapsed, in the midst of residential Swinton, (see 'Tunnel Vision' p. 65). The line never reopened and I never even knew of its existence as I trespassed beyond the limits of Clifton Junction Station.

Railway maps of Greater Manchester show many closures, but there still remains an extensive system. The Windsor Link will, for the first time, enable through running from, for example, Blackpool to Buxton, presently extremities of commuter services from Victoria for the former and from Piccadilly for the latter. Through trains from towns like Bolton and Blackburn to Piccadilly will inevitably bring a further retraction in the role of Victoria, itself a mere shadow of the once great complex 'double' station of Victoria and Exchange.

My visit to Oldham on an abysmal day in January 1966 produced a photograph, taken in the snow and featured in an earlier book, which baffled and defeated me when trying to ascertain its precise location. My respect for those who have the patience to read my books manifests itself in trying not to fool, mislead or misrepresent. Hence my frank admission of uncertainty as to where I was on that bleak day. My plea of ignorance was rewarded by numerous kind and informative letters

Re-covering my tracks: seen from Pepper Hill box the view had altered radically when I took this photograph in about 1980 (the diesel era blunts the interest in times and dates). The footbridge remains, but little else; and Pepper Hill box was demolished in 1986.

Whilst a longer lens alters the perspective, it is the symbolic reality of physical change in the environment nearly twenty years later that highlights the evident change in the landscape, as seen from my chosen eyrie. Now, at O/S 035783, the Manchester-Bolton line is over-ridden by the M62 motorway: no track, police, or signalling costs are being borne by the commercial traffic on it. I am afraid my 'interest' in diesels does not extend to recording their numbers, or knowing their class.

By the time that the 19.00 Manchester Victoria-Blackpool North train, hauled by Blackpool's 'Black Five' No 44819, passed Pepper Hill signal box, from the steps of which I shot this picture on 22 April 1964, the sun was low, there was not the benefit of today's fast colour film to 'freeze' one's subject and my panning was imperfect. The cooling towers of Agecroft Power Station are just visible in the right background, and Pilkington Tiles sidings are on the left.

In apologising for the quality of this photograph, its inclusion enables me to recall that, even at this date, a stream of well-filled steam-hauled commuter trains emerged from Victoria station to the erstwhile Lancashire cotton towns in the network built up by telling me precisely where I was. Let me thus again invite some helpful reader to tell me whether I am right or wrong in locating the photographs taken on 4 June 1968 and noted in my 'photo-bible' as 'View of severed Accrington to Bury line (L & Y)'; shots of the closed station, inside the tunnel, and of an abandoned goods shed are noted as being taken at Haslingden. But were they?

The line between Accrington and Stubbins opened on 17 August 1848, and saw its last passenger train in 1966. It was part of the 'main line' of the East Lancashire Railway (ELR) which was centred on Bury. At the time of its opening it was one of the most difficult lines to work anywhere in the country. It reached an altitude of 777ft above sea level between Haslingden and Baxenden, with gradients only fractionally less severe than the Lickey incline, whilst the trains, even in its later years, were worked by small tank engines. Incidentally, the line continued southwards through Bury to Molyneux Junction (and the LNWR line through Clifton Hall tunnel to Patricroft), and immediately thereafter to Clifton Junction where it joined the main line into Manchester, so my link with it justifies — to myself if nobody else — the reason for selecting it here.

Was I at Haslingden? Or was it Helmshore? If so, why? I can no longer remember whither I was bound. Haslingden station actually closed on 7 November 1960 although, as mentioned, passenger trains continued to use the Accrington-Bury line until 5 December 1966. Actual closure of the line from Accrington North Junction to Ramsbottom-Stubbins Junction was on that date, whilst the line from Stubbins Junction to Bury (Bolton Street) lingered on until 5 June 1972. On my Ordnance Survey map — 'Seventh Series No 95 Blackburn and Burnley', dated as 'Published 1961' — Baxenden Station is closed, but Haslingden is shown not only as open, which it was, but as a 'Principal Station', more a monument to its past history than to its contemporaneous situation.

Was I at Haslingden? Or was I at Helmshore? Maybe my five photographs were spread between the two. Close scrutiny of the photographs themselves shows a level crossing at the platform end. There was one at Helmshore but not at Haslingden. One shot is taken in a tunnel. There was a short tunnel at Haslingden, but not at Helmshore. In one of the photographs, my bald and bearded 'accomplice' (whose identity is a mystery these twenty years later) is pulling the signal wire to raise the alarm of the disused upper quadrant.

Not for the first time, and hopefully not for the last, the act of writing

the Lancashire & Yorkshire Railway. In steam days, the 17.40 (SX) Victoria to Bolton Trinity Street took sixteen minutes; today the 17.40 dmu takes twenty-five. In steam days the 18.10 (SX) Victoria to Wigan Wallgate arrived at 18.37; today, the 18.10 reaches Wigan Wallgate at 18.47. Anyone for steam . . . or do Manchester commuters really prefer this (below)? By August 1980, the scene from the steps of Pepper Hill box is markedly, but not totally, different. Obtrusive poles have appeared on the grass bank, but the cooling towers remain. Many journeys from Victoria to places like Blackburn, Bolton and Wigan were quicker in the steam era, as indicated in the caption.

books around my photographs mobilizes and goads me into researching the detail in the pictures. One final effort to solve the 'Haslingden or Helmshore Dilemma' has at last brought its reward. A small photograph in *Railways Around Lancashire* by A.C. Gilbert and N. R. Knight illustrates Haslingden Station. It is on a slight curve. My 'station' photograph cannot have been taken here. There is a goods shed, however, which could be that seen in one of the pictures. This 'negative' solution to my soliloquy was confirmed in a most exciting way half an hour later. Hopefully, I studied the 'Stations' section of *Lancashire and Yorkshire Railway Miscellany* by Noel Coates. There in Plates 90 and 91 is 'my' station: beyond doubt it is Helmshore. My photograph illustrates the view south towards Bury and Manchester. Although the old photographs in the *Miscellany* are undated, many features clearly determine the identity of my picture, probably taken some sixty years later, and, as can be seen, with the track still *in situ*. If only, if only, I had taken many more similar photographs.

For a chapter intended to feature the last stronghold of steam, and referring to Greater Manchester, I have trespassed both on geography and on your tolerance by rambling on about the Manchester-Bury-Accrington line, although keeping just within the bounds set by my

Few people bothered to photograph closed lines and stations in June 1968, let alone in colour; we were mostly too busy photographing the end of steam. Helmshore station, signals, signal box and level-crossing gates were still intact then. It was on the section of line which closed to passenger traffic on 5 December 1966, between Accrington and Ramsbottom, south of the famed and fearsome Baxenden Bank. A preservation scheme keeps hope alive here.

own loose discipline. Recently closed lines featured rarely in my photographic activities in steam's final years. Not surprisingly it was the locomotives themselves which were my target, and the remaining motive power depots became the focus both of my ambition and of my camera, together with Manchester Victoria and Exchange Stations. The former saw action almost until steam's final hour, and for me, supposedly 'on business' in Manchester, provided an accessible and convenient quick glimpse, or to use the jargon of today, 'quick fix'. It was a deal less harmful than some of the sights, sounds or substances that seem to be the source of contemporary interest or activity. But I digress.

As mentioned above, numerous excellent books have been written on the history of the railway in and around Manchester. No such task is attempted or suggested here. This is merely covering my tracks. From those early years of the Liverpool & Manchester Railway, the Oldham Alliance Railway, the East Lancashire Railway — the list is endless — the pre-grouping predominance was concentrated substantially in the hands of the Lancashire & Yorkshire and the London & North Western Railways, whose merger in 1922 formed in England the backbone, a year later, of the LMS. Whilst the erstwhile LNER had a presence in Manchester, there were few Eastern Region locomotives active by the time my photography started, although my first Manchester terminus photography, at Central in March 1963, included a Gorton (9G) 'B1' 4-6-0 No 61369, as mentioned earlier. Gorton, once the main workshops of the Great Central, latterly an LNER establishment, was transferred from Eastern to London Midland Region, the shed being 39A before becoming 9G on 23 February 1958. No 61369 was itself withdrawn in December 1963.

The final days of steam in Manchester were best recorded either at the L & Y's Newton Heath and the LNW's Patricroft sheds (9D and 9H respectively from 9 September 1963), or at the L & Y's Victoria or the LNW's Exchange Stations. Good weather often attended my visits to Manchester, but good fortune eluded me during some critical photography, particularly at Victoria and Exchange Stations in July and August 1967. My camera had been engaged in a tussle with Sam, our yellow labrador, who had undoubtedly had the better of the encounter, resulting in a maladjusted focusing system. By the time the fault was discovered and rectified, some 'wonderful' photographs turned out, on development, to be quite useless. Steam's days were ebbing away, my visits to Manchester were not unlimited, and to have had the photographs I took rendered useless by Sam's playfulness strained my canine fidelity somewhat. However, at Patricroft and Newton Heath there were no such problems, and I did manage a few worthwhile shots at Exchange and Victoria.

All too few colour photographs exist of steam at the great LNW/ L & Y complex that comprised these separate but attached stations.

On 10 August 1967, at the commencement of the last year of British steam, the 06.15 Heysham Boat Train has just arrived at Manchester Victoria station hauled by Carnforth's 'Black Five' 4-6-0 No 44874. Notwithstanding the size, importance and attraction of this station and contiguous Exchange, colour photographs here, as at Central, seem rare, albeit poor. The gloomy light provided wretched conditions for colour photography.

Travellers from Ireland disembark as the firemen puts the bag into the tender. The engine's cab seems to have filled with smoke, which appears to encompass it, as the safety valves lift gently. She survived until steam's final hour in August 1968.

The North Western's claim to be 'The Premier Line' speaks for itself. Few better descriptions of the importance of the LNWR exist than that imaginary description, by a mythical schoolmaster, as written by W.M. Acworth in his *magnum opus, The Railways of England.*

The North Western territory extends from London in the south to Carlisle in the north, and from Cambridge in the east to Swansea and Holyhead in the west — a distance of 300 miles in length by 200 miles in breadth. There are also two small outlying dependencies on the Irish coast, the one at the mouth of the Liffey, the other in Carlingford Lough. The seat of the government is at present in London, but the capital is Crewe, a town of 37,000 inhabitants consisting entirely of the employes (sic) of the Government and their families. The total number of the Civil Service does not fall far short of 60,000. The President is Sir Richard Moon, while his prime Minister, who is known by the title of General Manager, is George Findlay. The revenue of the annual budget, which last August flowed into the exchequer at the rate of £26 a minute, amounts to £10,000,000; and the funded debt is upwards of a hundred million pounds sterling.'

Acworth continues: 'It will be, we are persuaded, in some such words as these that, once the conservative mind of the British schoolmaster has awakened to the fact that counties and Lord Lieutenants are anachronisms, and that the United Kingdom has been divided and given to the great railway companies, the Board School pupil of the future will be taught his geography.'

Splendid fellow, Acworth! Those words, written in 1889, indicate the confidence and importance rightly attributed to the railway companies by a true enthusiast. As a politician writing almost a century later, I cannot but feel that recent attempts at local government reorganization, let alone transport policy, would best have been left to the likes of Acworth.

As can be seen from the map below, the tentacles of the LNWR spread well abroad around Manchester. The city was a vital cog in its operation. For the L & Y, however, Manchester was of even greater significance. Referring to that railway's contemporary developments in Manchester, Acworth says 'Londoners, who want to know what a local service can be, and ought to be, should go to Lancashire or Yorkshire and study the question'. Elsewhere he notes, in discussing timekeeping, 'The Lancashire and Yorkshire company has raised its standard all round; but then Lancashire and Yorkshire folk take improvements for granted...'

Central Manchester's railway system in 1888. Names have altered and much has changed, yet much remains. The new Windsor Link will run south, from a point near the L & Y Windsor Bridge Junction, to give direct rail access from Preston, Bolton etc into Piccadilly, here notated as 'London Road'.

Aligning the pictures in this chapter with this map, Trafford Park shed was on the Cheshire Lines Committee line from Liverpool into Manchester Central; Patricroft on the L & NW line from Liverpool into Exchange (and Victoria); Clifton Junction (Pepper Hill) on the L & Y from Preston, Bolton et al, through Pendleton into Victoria; whilst Newton Heath, in the top right-hand corner, served the L & Y lines north-eastwards from the city.

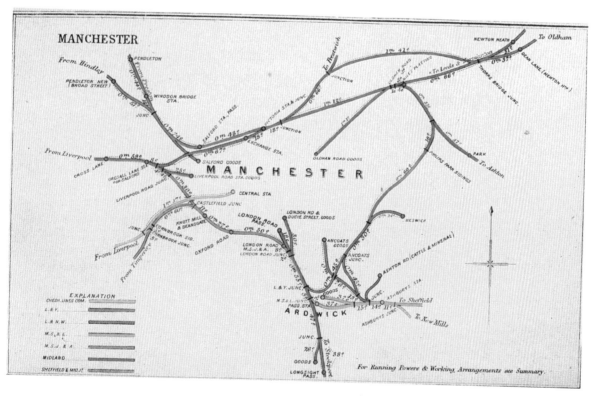

In comparing, whilst writing this chapter, the content of my photographs with those from earlier years, the most obvious and seemingly resilient feature is the partition wall alongside which the banking engines waited to assist eastbound trains up Miles Platting Bank. In September 1896, a Board of Trade report stated that traffic at the east end of Victoria Station was heavier than at any other point in England, yet the L & Y were still at that time being forced further to extend, culminating in the second LYR Act of 20 July 1986. Fortunately, railway architecture now receives the attention it is due, not only from railway enthusiasts but from those interested in history, town planning and archaeology. My intention here is merely to recall my own memories. The platform that joined Manchester's Victoria and Exchange Station was, at 2,194ft, the longest in Britain. However, by the time I arrived with my camera there was little steam left at the LNWR end. Exchange Station had already begun its decline, albeit newer (1884) than Victoria (1848). My lack of foresight resulted in failure to photograph these stations in their own right, rather that merely as a backdrop for steam.

Earlier in this Chapter I recorded my first visit to a Manchester terminus with a camera — to Central one night in March 1963. At this early stage of my mission to photograph the end of the steam era, my initiative had not extended to any of the city's motive power depots. My knowledge of, or indeed interest in, the subject of railway history *per se* was virtually non-existent. My memory now fails to respond to the question I ask myself as to why Patricroft was the first shed in Manchester to which I went. Perhaps it was information gleaned from that most excellent of publications, the *Railway Observer*, the journal of the Railway Correspondence and Travel Society. Or was it? Perusal, on writing these words, of the November and December 1964 issues of *RO* reveals no mention of Patricroft, and barely a mention even of Manchester. The December edition, however, yielded the following paragraph under BRITISH RAILWAYS — GENERAL:

'LOCOMOTIVE NAMEPLATES, etc — Swindon Works has for disposal a limited number of nameplates removed from locomotives of the Hall class. These are offered for sale at £15. 0s. 0d. each, subject to their remaining unsold. In addition, there are many brass cabside numberplates (£7. 10s. 0d. each, free-on-rail Swindon) and also cast-iron cabside number plates (£1. 0s. 0d. each, free-on-rail Swindon), carriage charges payable by the purchaser. Anyone interested in the purchase of any of these items should write to Stores Controller, Swindon, Wilts.'

What, you might ask, has all this to do with Patricroft, or Manchester? Nothing really, save only that it provides me with an opportunity to pay homage to those who compiled for posterity through the pages of the *Railway Observer* the detailed history of the end of steam. In the midst of the section on the London Midland region in that edition of December 1964 are some splendid photographs from an RCTS 'Tour of Eastern Europe, 28th August–14th September 1964', and the writing of this actual paragraph was interrupted by my own brief visit to Hungary in November 1986. Let us, however, return to Manchester; the *RO* has a single-sentence entry on the city in the December 1964 issue — 'MANCHESTER: BR 2-6-2T 84015, ex-shops in unlined black, was banking at Manchester Victoria on 29th October'.

The wall alongside which the Miles Platting bank engines waited, to which I referred earlier, remains for me an abiding feature of the end of the steam era in the city of Manchester. Snatched visits to Newton Heath and Patricroft sheds, usually in fine weather, are my other lasting recollections.

Newton Heath MPD was situated on what was an open site on the edge of the city, due to overcrowding of the original site at Miles Platting where, even by 1875, more than a hundred locomotives were allocated alongside the company's works. In 1876 Newton Heath shed was opened adjacent to the L & Y's carriage and wagon works. With twenty-four roads the shed was immense in comparison to many depots and was the largest engine shed on the Lancashire & Yorkshire

Standing proud and erect outside Newton Heath shed on 3 December 1964, Southport (8M) 'Black Five' 4-6-0 No 45375 surely epitomizes the lure of the steam engine. Note the splendid water-column, an incidental feature in numerous shed photographs. This Lancashire & Yorkshire specimen would be a truly valuable item of railway industrial archaeology today — have any such specimens survived?

No 45375, albeit workstained, would doubtless have served, with hundreds of her sisters, decades beyond the date of peremptory withdrawal which, in her case, was from Liverpool Edge Hill in January 1968. She was cut up at Cohen's, Kettering, in July that year.

Railway; its allocation at the peak of steam operations reached nearly 200 engines.

Naturally, over the years, as locomotives grew in size so the facilities were enlarged, the turntables being an obvious candidate as Barton Wright machines gave way to Stanier varieties. Such was the acreage of the place that the second turntable was actually nearer to Dean Lane Station than to Newton Heath. As 'LMS' became 'BR', so in turn BR Standard and Austerity locomotives were allocated. As steam declined, engines were concentrated in the northern half of the depot. On my visit there on 3 December 1964, albeit restricted by time, the classes that I photographed were:

'WD' 2-8-0	'Crab' 2-6-0
'4F' 0-6-0	'9F' 2-10-0
'3F' 0-6-0T	Ivatt 2-6-0
'Black Five' 4-6-0	

In addition, I was fortunate to capture a named 'B1' on an empty stock train passing the shed travelling east. Although this was the only visit I was able to make, the memory remains clear, particularly of those splendid L & Y water columns, of which twelve once stood sentry alongside the twenty-four shed roads. Newton Heath was one of the last steam sheds to survive on BR, finally closing on 1 July 1968. Demolition began the following March.

Whilst inevitably it is the LNWR and L & Y which dominated the railway scene in Manchester, the Midland Railway could not be excluded altogether; indeed, the L & Y regarded that railway as an ally in its battles with the North Western. Thus, through complex traffic arrangements, the description of which is beyond the scope of this chapter, the Midland, through its part ownership of the Cheshire Lines Committee (CLC) equally with the Great Northern and Great Central, obtained a firm foothold in Manchester. Trafford Park shed, opened in March 1895, was the largest depot on the CLC system, and was originally shared jointly by two of the three CLC partners, the MR and GCR, the GN taking its share of space just before the turn of the century. At the 1923 grouping, Great Northern and Great Central interest was vested in the LNER, whilst the Midland, the L & Y and its great rival the LNW, were merged into the LMS.

Notwithstanding that two of the three CLC partners were thus LNER constituents, Trafford Park, with its twenty roads, gradually became more and more identified with the LMS and latterly the London Midland Region of BR. In 1950 it acquired its own district, coded 13A, and became responsible for former MR and CLC sheds in the area; this was but a short-lived interregnum, and by May that year, in spite of its allocated stock of LNER engines, it was placed by BR into the London Midland Region firmament by being coded 9E. History, however, especially railway history, is not easily eradicated. For reasons

which I have not fully researched, the shed in January 1957 was removed from the Manchester district and transferred to that of Derby, erstwhile headquarters of the Midland Railway. That did not last long, its 17F coding reverting to 9E on transfer back to administration from Manchester in April 1958. The shed was still providing motive power for the former Midland main line services from Manchester Central to St Pancras, as well as the passenger duties on former Great Central (and Great Northern) rosters for which GCR locomotives were still allocated; the last of these were not withdrawn until the final decade of steam.

By the time I paid my only visit to Trafford Park shed, on 21 December 1967, motive power was restricted to Stanier '8F' 2-8-0s and 'Black Five' 4-6-0s, unkempt and in keeping with their surroundings. Visible signs of the shed's multi-company heritage were not apparent. That part of the shed that was covered was clad in corrugated sheeting of BR vintage. Lamps were suspended from arms off wooden posts, four lamps to each featureless post. Alongside the retaining wall

The water-tower and coaling apparatus are partly visible in this shot of '8F' 2-8-0 No 48317 taken on 21 December 1967, at Trafford Park shed. Camera problems and poor light are evident.

This shed served the Cheshire Lines Committee line from Manchester to Liverpool, and was the largest shed on the CLC system; it finally closed on 4 March 1968. No 48317, at this date allocated to Trafford Park — as painted on the buffer-beam — survived only three months more, succumbing to the breakers at Draper's, Hull, in August 1968.

Opposite *Patricroft shed was an odd shape. Here, on 5 March 1965, LMS '3F' 0-6-0T No 47378 provides another reminder of the atmosphere, gone and irreplaceable, of the engine shed in the steam era. The scene today is totally unrecognizable, a 'light industrial estate' — that euphemism for a faceless sprawl of characterless corrugated shacks, huts and cheaply-constructed units — having replaced the two shed buildings at this triangular site. The former LNWR Manchester-Liverpool line, which is barely visible at the extreme left of this photograph, is still there; so, just, is Patricroft station, just discernible to the left of the Jinty's bunker. The wagons in the right background stand on the stump of the Patricroft-Clifton Junction line (see 'Tunnel Vision'): it crossed the LNWR line from Eccles Junction (see the map on page 64) to Tyldesley and Bolton, which formed the third side of the triangle. Searching for remains of the railway at Patricroft at this point necessitates negotiating the line of the M62 motorway. My advice — don't bother, it is too depressing.*

No 47378, at home at Patricroft at this date, was withdrawn in November 1965 and cut up at Ward's, Killamarsh, the following February. If she was around today, I should like to put her on some track outside the Swansea Holiday Inn, itself being built on the site of the former LNWR/LMS shed at Paxton Street.

was the coal stage, with a chain belt providing the means of filling locomotive tenders. Someone, I recall not who, kindly photographed me on the buffer-beam of '8F' No 48317, incongruously dressed in tweed suit with waistcoat — me, not the '8F'. Thus, between business calls, was I able only to pay snatched visits to such places. The light was good, but my camera was not, suffering from that knock which affected the focus and which I was not to discover until after this visit to Manchester and to Trafford Park shed and signal box, which feature in a couple of sadly out-of-focus shots on that watery winter day. The shed closed on 4 March 1968, just over two months after my visit; the site is now obliterated.

Although I was able to take a few photographs at Bolton shed as late as 25 June 1968, by which time inevitably only 'Black Fives' and '8F's were in steam, it is to Patricroft that my final thoughts were directed. Today, Patricroft is merely a station on the former LNWR Liverpool-Manchester main line, and the station is itself a sad shadow of its former self. Long gone is the Patricroft-Molyneux Junction line of 1850 (see 'Tunnel Vision', p. 64). Likewise the other arm of the triangle, the Eccles Junction to Springs Branch Junction line of 1864, let alone the forgotten spur from the latter to the former. Of the shed there is nothing; a far cry from that day when, armed with my copy of *The British Locomotive Shed Directory* I followed the instructions:

'PATRICROFT
The shed is in the fork of the Eccles-Patricroft and Eccles-Monton Green lines. The yard is partially visible from both lines.
  Turn left outside Patricroft Station along a narrow road running parallel to the railway, and continue into Hampden Grove. A footbridge leads from the left-hand side of this road to the shed. Walking time 5 minutes.'

I do not recommend you to attempt such a fruitless journey today, save only to savour the unrecognizable landscape.

Opened by the LNWR on 1 January 1885, Patricroft shed was a manifestation of the rapidly-developing railway infrastructure in Manchester. Sited on virgin land, it was intended to cope with the increasing demand for motive power facilities resulting from overstretched capacity at Longsight and Ordsall Lane depots. It was not far from Agecroft shed, an L & Y depot, the construction of which was also the result of rapid traffic growth. Both Agecroft and Patricroft were intended primarily as freight locomotive depots, and both were adjacent to extensive goods yards.

Within the secure bounds of its own triangular site, Patricroft was eminently suitable for extension, and its accessibility from different sides resulted in the eventual extension, opened in about 1904, being constructed at right-angles to the original shed — a most unusual

development, and not one which to my knowledge existed anywhere else. Over the years considerable changes and improvements were made both by the LMS and indeed by BR, who rebuilt and re-roofed the 'old' shed.

As can be seen from the list overleaf of the locomotives that I photographed, the 'Britannia' and 'Jubilee' Classes appeared at Patricroft in the shed's declining years, regularly having brought trains from North Wales into Manchester. Checking the details of these engines, however, is fascinating. No 45657 *Tyrwhitt*, dead inside the shed's recesses on 1 December 1964, was actually transferred to Patricroft from Bank Hall, Liverpool, the previous May. Clearly Patricroft's shedmaster had not intended it for martyrdom, for the engine was actually withdrawn in September, and would, soon after my photograph was taken, be despatched on her final journey to the Central Wagon Company at Ince, Wigan, where she was scrapped. My photographs on 5 March 1965 of 'Jubilee' No 45647 *Sturdee* and of 'Britannia' 70022 *Tornado* were of 'foreign' machines, based at that date at Farnley Junction and Carlisle Upperby respectively. It would be interesting to enquire on what workings they arrived into Manchester — perhaps some kind reader will inform me? *Sturdee* was one of the last 'Jubilees' to survive, being withdrawn in April 1967.

Patricroft's 70ft turntable was installed during LMS days. It was sited strategically adjacent to both old and new sheds, as can be seen in

Opposite *Inevitably, at the very end of steam, variety in motive power was lacking; but engines other than 'Black Fives' and '8Fs' were abundant in the mid-sixties. On 1 December 1964, Hughes-Fowler 'Crab' 2-6-0 No 42734 from 9B Stockport was manoeuvring around Patricroft shed yard. Patricroft was the LNWR shed, but forty-two years after the LNWR/LYR merger, this 'Crab' was hardly an interloper. Sturdy northern reliability, deeds not words, were the 'Crab's' contribution to the British motive power scene. The 245 members of the class were amongst the most reliable of locomotives, and the distinctive chimney, with its Lancashire & Yorkshire heritage, earned my special affection.*

No 42734 and I had a similar career pattern at this time. She was transferred from Stockport to 8H Birkenhead in 1965 at around the date of my adoption as prospective Conservative Parliamentary Candidate there. I lost in March 1966 — the month she was withdrawn.

Patricroft, with its 'new' shed building at right-angles to the 'old', was in a triangle which contained extensive sidings. Engine movements, even at this late date, were abundant. Note the water tank over the former coal stage.

the accompanying plan. I was fortunate enough to obtain a good shot of an engine on the 'table', BR Standard '4' 4-6-0 No 75010, a visitor from Chester MPD, on 1 December 1964. Are there any other colour photographs of a locomotive on Patricroft's turntable?

The reference in the 'Shed Directory' to 'narrow road' and 'footbridge' inevitably brings back memories of the thrill — there is no other word — inherent in approaching a big locomotive depot in the steam era. For today's enthusiast there is no comparable experience. The nostrils twitched, the eyes and ears strained and the nerves jangled, especially if, in the absence of a shed pass, you were reliant on your wit to gain entry and to take photographs. Patricroft shed, with its strategic position within that fork of the junction — the Molyneux Junction line was long gone by the date of my visits to the Manchester area — provided excellent opportunities for 'straying' from within the strict confines of the shed itself on to the adjacent lines on which there was still work for steam motive power in late 1964 and early 1965.

To a young man, the cost of colour film then precluded the random, even careless (cost-wise) photography which I practise nowadays, so one can only curse and bemoan the shots one did not take; nevertheless, my records show a reasonable variety of motive power on shed at this late date. My notes indicate thus:

'Crab' 2-6-0	'3F' 0-6-0T
'Jubilee' 4-6-0	BR Standard
	'5' and
	Caprotti '5' 4-6-0
'Black Five' 4-6-0	
'8F' 2-8-0	'Britannia' 4-6-2

To these seven classes, add the four listed on page 166 at Newton Heath

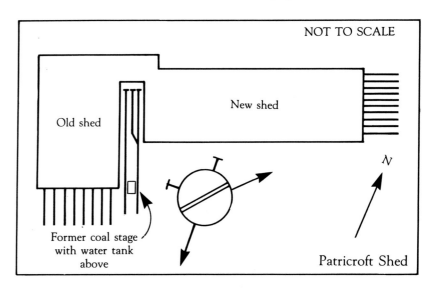

NOT TO SCALE

Old shed

New shed

Former coal stage with water tank above

N

Patricroft Shed

and not duplicated at Patricroft. Then let me note and add the classes I photographed at the other Manchester locations, eliminating duplications:

Manchester Central
  'B1' 4-6-0
  Fairburn '4MT' ⎫
  Stanier '4MT' ⎭ 2-6-4T
Clifton Junction
  Stanier '5MT' 2-6-0
  Fowler '4F' 0-6-0

Thus I was fortunate enough to photograph sixteen different classes of steam engine in the Manchester area, an area of probably unrivalled variety in its railway history and heritage.

To start a chapter such as this is simple. To round it off is less so. The memories remain, as do the eternal pangs, bred of ignorance and of opportunity lost. Manchester — the single word encompasses an almost endless variety of railway activity: Guide Bridge and Glossop; Oldham; Salford and the Ship Canal; Woodhead; the Liverpool & Manchester; Bury and Bacup; Horwich and Blackrod — the names flood and flow. Manchester, Lancashire — railway history incarnate.

Let me end by taking you to Eccles, the Patricroft Triangle and the memories of those junctions, bridges, stations, signal boxes of yesterday, for in truth this is a personal choice and my memories of experience rather than my imaginings through knowledge gleaned from books is all that I can offer that can claim your attention. To enable me to end this chapter, I thus returned to Manchester on a bleak, November morning. But before recovering these tracks, let me spend a moment soliloquizing about this corner of Greater Manchester.

The spawning railways of the early Victorian years reached out into the countryside beyond the city of Manchester. Where railways went, suburbs followed. By the end of the nineteenth century, the railway map of Lancashire looked like the meanderings of a drunken spider. Eccles, on the original Liverpool-Manchester line (see the map on page 64), is associated with the first railway fatality, for it was here that the Duke of Wellington stopped to enquire about William Huskisson. The first of the two junctions from L & M at Eccles ran, as already mentioned, from the east end of Patricroft station to Molyneux Junction. Opened in 1850, it gave access to the East Lancashire Railway. The second junction, half a mile east of Patricroft, was opened on 1 September 1864 by the LNWR. It ran to Springs Branch, Wigan. Thus was created Patricroft Triangle, within which was Patricroft Shed, with its turntable, clearly visible on my 1954 OS map. The 1977 map, however, tells its own tale of decline. Gone are the junctions, track and railway buildings. No doubt ere long that distinctive white triangle of land will itself be subsumed under more unmemorable suburban architecture.

'Industrial Archaeology' is an appropriate phrase to trace the changes in the landscape hereabouts. To many people 'archaeology' means ancient Greece or Rome, Egypt or China. This can be both expensive, restrictive and inadequate for those whose interest is in British industrial archaeology and who seek at short notice and with little available time to pursue a specific search for our railway heritage. Let us, during this soliloquy, pause for a moment to consider the implications of generating interest amongst a broader public of 'railway archaeology' as a subject. Archaeology, according to the Oxford Dictionary, is the 'study of antiquities, esp. of the prehistoric period'. 'Prehistory' is 'of the period antecedent to history'. 'History' is the 'continuous methodical record of public events', then the 'whole train of events connected with nation, person, thing, etc. eventful past career . . .'. On that basis, my intention to end this chapter on an archaeological note is an eminently acceptable description of my interest. Let me return from soliloquy to reality.

My return to Patricroft on 25 November 1986 was a deliberate step. Between this date and my last visit more than twenty-one years earlier, the railway map of the area, and indeed of Lancashire, has been fundamentally eroded. The formidable web of lines linking Manchester with the main towns, and those towns with each other, has been severed. With their demise and with the end of steam have gone the engine sheds and their ancillary buildings, most of the signal boxes, the viaducts, the bridges, the tunnels, cuttings and embankments that personified the willingness and determination of our Victorian forebears to fund one of the most extensive and effective transportation systems ever built. That system was itself the precursor of the 'history' of that area, for now so much is but a memory. Who, though, has yet seen fit to undertake a thorough 'study of the antiquities' of the railway era hereabouts?

Not surprisingly, some features of the bygone railway age are more likely than others to attract attention. Books on the railway in the landscape, on utilizing disused lines as long-distance footpaths, are becoming quite common. Many buildings and some structures are now put to alternative use, but others have gone, unrecorded, unloved and sadly unremembered. As the motorways swept through Manchester they helped to obliterate landmarks created with the blood, sweat, toil and tears of the Victorians. Let us spare a moment to reflect; I choose two tunnels, perhaps the most difficult of all forms of railway infrastructure to put to alternative use, or obliterate. Or are they?

Undoubtedly the greatest tunnelling achievement in the region was Woodhead. Inevitably, controversy and rivalry attended the birth of the early railways. The Sheffield, Ashton-under-Lyne & Manchester Railway, under the chairmanship of Lord Wharncliffe, was no exception. The company was incorporated by its Act of Parliament of 5 May 1837. Lord Wharncliffe cut the first sod near the Woodhead end of the proposed tunnel. Vignoles, the original engineer-in-chief, cut the second. Vignoles resigned his office at the end of 1839 to be succeeded by the great Joseph Locke, who soon realized that Vignoles' estimates of the cost of Woodhead Tunnel were woefully inadequate. As we whisk, at great speed and in comfort, through BR's main-line tunnels today, do we spare a thought for the men who designed and built them? Few do. Who, travelling through the sootless double-bore tunnel which replaced the original Woodhead Tunnel when the line was electrified (and which itself is now closed), could imagine the Board of Trade Inspector, General Parley, inspecting the original single-line bore by fiery torchlight on 20 December 1845? The General pronounced it to be one of the finest pieces of engineering he had ever seen; as Hamilton Ellis wrote, in *British Railway History 1830-1876*, this was 'a quaint compliment to Locke, who had carried it out and who hated tunnels'. Two days later, a vital link in Manchester's railway network was completed with the arrival via Woodhead tunnel of the inaugural train on the first direct railway run from Sheffield.

The odd and often mysterious nature of tunnels with their nocturnal environment, is captured in Hamilton Ellis' words: 'So Woodhead Tunnel was with us. Nobody had ever loved it. From the first, it caused the railway to suffer from a nightmare of tracheal and colonic complications, while, regarding the humanities, Mr Dow, in his neat history of the railway, has recorded a Victorian opinion, which likened the taste of the air therein to cheap port. Certainly, its brimstone bouquet had knocked down many people during the ensuing century and more. Only electrification and replacement could cure the enormities of Woodhead Tunnel, and these the late London & North Eastern Railway Company set about carrying into being'.

Neither electrification nor replacement has been the lot of other tunnels, which merit a chapter to themselves; but this chapter is about Manchester, so it is one of the few tunnels within Greater Manchester, and the line which it covered, to which we turn our attention, and to which I made reference earlier in 'Tunnel Vision'. On Tuesday 25 November 1986, spurred on with the incentive to complete this chapter, I set out to seek the remains of the Eccles triangle, the Patricroft Junctions and Clifton Hall Tunnel. It was a nostalgic but melancholy reunion, made more interesting and infinitely more enjoyable in the company of John Brownlow, whom I met by prior arrangement at Warrington (see pages 65-71).

It is all an age ago now from the time when the phrase 'East Lancs Road' was synonymous with fast motoring 'twixt Liverpool and Manchester. Representing a constituency in a county without an inch of motorway, the web thereof which spreads around Manchester at least belies the myth about imbalance of infrastructural expenditure in our country. Lack of familiarity with road developments can cause havoc with one's memory. Thus, it was but a few minutes after joining the M5 outside Warrington that we were crossing Chat Moss; railway history began to close in on us. We spotted Barton Moss signal box standing gaunt against the lightening sky; as we threaded a motorway interchange, queues of stationary cars paid their own silent tribute to the advantages of an effective and efficient urban railway system.

Having decided, in the limited time available, to start my 'journey of remembrance' at Patricroft, we came off whichever motorway we were on — how dull and individually characterless are roads when compared to railways, and I refer not to the scenery — we found ourselves at a roundabout and John asked me if I would like to drop in to Eccles signal box. That is like asking a small boy if he would like a gob-stopper, so we eased our way alongside two hovering traffic cops, descended a ramp from the road to the railway line — and there in front of us was Eccles box.

We were in another world. From the frantic menagerie of the motorway and the motor car, where reckless speed, sprawl, disorder and ill manners are the order of the day, we entered the dignified and organized world of the railway. Although my Mancunian meanderings had brought me to the vicinity more than twenty years previously, this was my first visit to Eccles box; with its levers and bells it would probably have been clearly recognizable to a Victorian visitor reawakened from years spent in a time capsule. Inevitably, my thoughts turned to the immense scale of the task of modernization undertaken by British Rail in the last few years, and yet to be completed. Why do we set such disparate safety standards as between road and rail? Why do we insist that passenger and freight trains must be subject to signalling discipline and distance between vehicles, whilst passenger and freight vehicles of the internal combustion engine variety are subject to no such restraints? More than 5,000 corpses annually, and more than a quarter of a million maimed and mangled bodies attest to the utter extremities of safety and regard for life and limb which characterize the disparate laws we impose, without logic, on road and rail travel. Why do we so differentiate? If the same attitude to safety prevailed — and why, pray, should they not? — then untold families would not now mourn their loved ones where lives have been sacrificed on the altar of 'convenience' that seems to be the guiding star of those who make the rules of travel by internal combustion engine.

These were the thoughts that engulfed me as we left Eccles box and rejoined the frantic world above the cutting. Eccles is on the original Liverpool & Manchester Railway, and the pioneer line's arterial significance was brought to mind as train numbers 1M56 and 1E94, respectively the 06.51 York to Liverpool and the 08.03 Liverpool to Newcastle, thundered through Eccles Station. The opening of the L & M in September 1830 was truly the beginning of a social and commercial revolution. The relationship between the railway and the waterways they replaced, and between the internal combustion engine and the railway, which it diminished but has not replaced, could form the basis for a thesis beyond the scope of this modest tome. In Britain, our railways have survived and passed their nadir. More motorways now seem to mean more congestion, and in Manchester deregulation of bus services has, as I write these words, coincided with a small but significant upsurge in rail traffic on certain routes. As John Brownlow and I set out from Eccles down the road in search of the erstwhile rail triangle, he told me that trains on the Bury line were now loading to passenger levels not seen for more than twenty years.

What can I say about the site of the Patricroft triangle? My memory recalled BR Caprotti '5' 4-6-0s on lengthy rakes of coal empties returning north-west from Manchester. Patricroft shed was a pivotal point in these activities. One could ramble on indefinitely about those long gone days of steam-hauled freight and passenger trains, but there is no point in it all — one is just left with sad memories. Patricroft was part of the last stronghold of steam in Britain. The best of it now is a featureless wasteland; the rest of it part of the concrete jungle of motorway-dominated suburbia. With steam went a much more personal way of life — not just in Manchester, but over our whole railway system.

MAKING TRACKS

Since time immemorial, until the coming of the railway, man's speed and scope of movement on land had been restricted to the ability of the fastest horse or camel to cover the greatest distance in the shortest time. With the coming of the 'iron horse', man's horizons quite literally disappeared. The railway age indeed heralded a brave new world: the prerogative of travel was no longer restricted to the powerful or wealthy. Railways created towns; junctions appeared in the middle of the countryside; great stations, bridges, tunnels and viaducts were erected; and of course the steam engine gave birth to a cult of proportions unimagined to our early Victorian forebears.

Britain's railway history is the richest in the world. Indeed, the drama, struggle and intrigue of the early railway years make life today seem tame and unadventurous. However, the purpose of this chapter is not to write a potted history, but to try to illustrate with word and picture the impact of the railway on the countryside. Perhaps before we proceed further, I may be excused for deciding — call it author's licence if you will — that 'countryside' means town and country. My selection of 'tracks revisited' is random, and merely a fraction of the total.

Perhaps the simplest means of illustrating the environmental appeal of railways is to compare them to roads, and to contrast the attitude of affection and sentimentality felt by millions towards the steam engine with the views of hostility held equally strongly by millions towards the caravan. The current controversy aroused by the proposed closure of the great Settle to Carlisle railway line, with its magnificent Ribblehead viaduct, is generated only in small part by 'transport' rather than by aesthetic considerations. Railways enhance the landscape; roads desecrate it. Steam engines struggling bravely up steeply inclined lines epitomize man's battle with and supremacy over the elements. Streams of motor cars towing dishwashing machines better illustrate this point than that scar across Cumbria called the M6. It is wretched compared to its rail predecessor, the great trunk line of the London & North Western Railway over Shap Fell and through the Lune Gorge.

That roads open up new areas to tourism is often adduced as their sole or main justification; yet 'motor tourism' is a phenomenon that has a debit as well as a credit side on the balance sheet of tourism.

Visitors who came by rail often stayed longer, and did not demand space in which to drive and park their vehicles. The decline of the rail holiday is directly attributable to the growth in numbers of the motoring public. The struggle for supremacy of rail versus road is inexorable. Currently, the journey from Fort William to Mallaig can be seen as a case in point. Scenically one of Britain's finest railway lines, the West Highland Extension has disappeared as a freight artery. Fish traffic that was formerly a sinecure of the railway, now moves by road, and huge trucks, quite unsuitable for the narrow lane that is called the A830, hurtle along a highway that was neither designed nor intended for the juggernaut. However, as I write these words there comes news that fish traffic on the Malaig line has surprisingly and happily been won back by British Rail from under the noses of the road hauliers. The little Inverness-shire village could soon be forwarding a shipload of palletized fish every week. That British Rail's policy during the past twenty years was, however, a factor in its transfer from rail to road cannot be denied. That the true costs — social and environmental as well as financial — are loaded in favour of road and against rail cannot be denied either.

Yet the line to Mallaig survives, and even prospers, as those responsible for tourism begin successfully to extol the virtues of a rail

Somehow this delightful shunting cabin has survived, near the site of New England engine shed in Peterborough, and was photographed on 12 June 1986 whilst I was inspecting the East Coast Main Line electrification work. The British Rail system is still well stocked with edifices of this vintage, many indeed dating back into the last century. Students of railway history have spread their gaze well beyond the motive power department, and railway architecture is a subject in its own right; will somebody photograph and document the remaining signal cabins, many of which are distinctive examples of the style of the pre-grouping railways?

The 'Race to the North' was fought, won and lost at this point on the railway map of Britain — Kinnaber Junction signal box, photographed in May 1982. I obtained for local preservationists the offer of a substantial grant from the Scottish Tourist Board for the removal of the box and its rebuilding at nearby Brechin; but my — and the STB's — offer was neglected.

A considerable feat of imagination is required in looking at this photograph to visualize 'A4s' sweeping round the bend off the Strathmore line as recently as the 1960s, at the head of the Glasgow-Aberdeen three-hour expresses. The distinctive multiple telegraph-poles are rapidly disappearing from Britain's landscape.

journey as an end in itself. Not far away, separated by Ben Nevis, the haunting wastelands of Rannoch Moor are best felt and seen from the lonely line that threads that treacherous land of bog, peat and moss.

Lest it should be thought that my heart lingers longer in Scotland than elsewhere, or that remoteness is a necessary ingredient in locating and appreciating the railway, let me bring you south to one of the fastest growing, most prosperous and crowded parts of Britain. If you feel, as do I, that the M4 motorway between Reading and Slough lacks charm, try the railway. Have you ever spent a day in Sonning Cutting? Here, a short flit from the M4, the A4 and the crowded hustle of towns which bring out the most excruciating adjectives from estate agents, you can watch the trains go by and collect unsurpassed *fraises-du-bois*. Mind you, it is not the same without steam. To stand beside the track, watching the signals, and then to see that first wisp of steam in the distance was an exhilarating experience for a railway enthusiast.

Perhaps the least considered aspect of the decline of the railway is its effect on the cartography of the countryside. It is a wistful experience to revisit the site of a once-known line, but it is historically both instructive and nostalgic to recall the fate of railway lines on Ordnance Survey maps. To my mind it is impossible fully to enjoy, appreciate and explore Britain without OS. When a line was in service, the stations were marked with large red dots. When the stations close, the dots become white, empty circles — devoid of colour. Then the track is lifted and the map bears the legend 'Tk of old Rly'. Finally, as the years pass, the line becomes broken up by development, and 'Cse of old Rly' is all that remains. Physical reminders of the railway of yesteryear will linger, but not, perhaps, for ever.

Once there was a great gasometer overlooking the old Midland Railway engine shed at Barrow Road in Bristol; indeed, for those fortunate enough to have visited this Mecca of steam in years gone by, the gasometers were the landmark, nay the geographical trademark, of the last home of steam in that great city. The gasometers outlived the steam engine. The site of Barrow Road shed, right in the heart of Bristol, is now a little-visited wilderness of willow-herb, groundsel and buddleia. The last steam engine left Barrow Road in October 1965, nearly one hundred and twenty years after the Midland Railway had leased the small shed previously erected on the site by the Bristol & Gloucester railway.

Bristol has always been an important railway centre, and was a meeting place of the Great Western and Midland Railways. The former built a huge cathedral of steam at St Philips Marsh. What a place it was: a huge, towering roundhouse in which, like gentle dragons at rest, the off-duty masterpieces of Churchward and his successors rested between duties. St Philips Marsh shed closed on 15 June 1964, and Great Western engines (they *were* Great Western, not merely Western Region) were transferred across the city to Barrow Road, which enjoyed a miraculous, overcrowded few weeks of hectic activity. Nothing better illustrates the decline and demise of the railway than the appalling, boring, tasteless buildings that now desecrate the site of St Philips Marsh shed. I have photographed them, but they are revolting and dull, like the tinned and packaged supermarket fodder inside the warehouse now

This chapter has endless photographic alternatives. The Clifton Extension Railway in Bristol is recalled by this sign I photographed in September 1971. Where is it now?

occupying this once hallowed site. It is certainly not worth showing the 'after' of a 'before-and-after' here.

One place where the railway does remain a dominant feature of the landscape is Crewe. From the moment that the Grand Junction Railway's works was moved here from Edge Hill, its importance on the railway map of Britain was assured. Branches to Chester and Manchester were an early sprouting of the many-branched trunk lines of what became the great London & North Western Railway. That arrival of the Grand Junction's works saw an influx of 800 men, women and children in March 1843. By 1848 more than 1,000 men were employed at Crewe Works. The town, which grew directly from the railway, was laid out by Joseph Locke, whilst the railway spawned associated industries and was responsible for the growth in population from 19,000 in 1871 to 29,000 in 1891 and to 45,000 in 1911. Referring to the role of the LNWR, Professor Jack Simmons, in his splendid book *The Railway in Town and Country* refers, somewhat blandly, however, to the fact that 'The company also gave the town the Queens Park, a Jubilee tribute, opened in 1888'. That, however, was not quite how Bill Taylor told me the tale when I went searching for the railway heritage in Crewe on Monday 24 November 1986. My visit was at the invitation of Colin Evans, Managing Director of Chester Barrie, whose factory was, perhaps, home to the ghosts of the clothing factory built by the LNWR of John Compton in the 1850s and whose firm made uniforms for its staff.

Colin Evans is a thoroughly modern businessman running a successful company in Crewe, but even he is not immune to the pervasive history of the railway. When I asked him to try to arrange for me to meet a railwayman amongst, or retired from, his staff who could give me a first-hand account of 'Crewe the Railway Town', he took me personally to the home of Bill Taylor.

Few people today could have greater personal experiences of the LNWR to relate than has Bill Taylor. He joined the LNWR in 1918, and was employed in the Works, in the forge and on the steam hammer. 'Charles John Bowen-Cooke was the boss, and everyone knew it. Tim Savage made the wheels and tyres. He was manager of the steel works, and the wheels were made there until about the time I joined the company. Mind you, nobody used Christian names — in them days they were "Sir". Bill Taylor talked and I scribbled as hard and fast as possible, regretting my inability to write shorthand. From the forge, he transferred to the iron foundry; this was in 1926, by which time the LNWR had been merged into the LMS. Then in that year he lost an eye; he was transferred to the locomotive offices, and was appointed a Crewe Works Guide. 'On the LNWR we started at 6 am — on the LMS it was 7.55.' (That this change resulted from trade union activity, rather than workers' enthusiasm for the LNWR, should not be allowed to spoil the story.)

Crewe rarely features in books of railway nostalgia, not least because the railway still thrives at the headquarters of the LNWR. That railway's heroes are commemorated around the town, but history rather than scenery provides the memorable backdrop. On the corners of mean streets are immortalized the great men, public and lesser-known, of the LNWR. Of the memory of the company's Chief Mechanical Engineers, none has better stood the test of time than that of Charles John Bowen-Cooke, CME from 1909 to 1920.

With 136½ acres of Works, Bill is proud of the fact that he was guide to what he describes as 'the largest railway works in the world'. As he tells the tale, however, the gift of Queens Park to the town of Crewe by the LNWR in 1888 had little to do with philanthropy. 'The company wanted to keep the GWR out of the town, so it brought up this land and presented it to the town on condition that it was kept for the people for ever, and no railway was to be built on any of it.' (The GWR had running powers into Crewe from Wellington.)

The LNWR has, frankly, little of which to be too proud in relation to the heritage of Crewe. However, a wander round some of the older streets will reveal magical reminders of the great men of the LNWR. Bowen-Cooke and Webb — names with which to conjure for any enthusiast — are commemorated on the corner of mean streets that call to mind the typicality of Victorian urban development.

For the *aficionados* of LNWR history, Edelston Road in Crewe will call to mind the name of the family who sold much of the land to the railway, land sold for very little due to its clay consistency. Merrills Building is named after the farmer who also owned the land. Crewe retains its railway, and honours the great and lesser-known names of the past. It is a town of memories.

Another wistful site today is Feltham, once the busy location of the large marshalling yard of the London and South Western Railway. Unlike Crewe, it has neither history, nor heritage, nor living memories of its previous significance. With an engine shed incorporated into this suburban railway centre, Feltham and steam were for me synonymous. Now, only the wind disturbs the weeds and rattles the remains of derelict buildings long since devoid of life.

Perhaps the best-loved railway of them all was, and indeed still is, the Somerset & Dorset Joint Railway. Built to link the Bristol and English Channels, it cut an individualistic swathe through Great Western territory, yet was owned jointly by the Midland and London & South Western Railways. It was always an individual, indeed singular, line. In its heyday, its traffic varied from coal from the Somerset coalfields to heavy through holiday trains from Midland and Northern towns and cities to Bournemouth, the most famous of which, the 'Pines Express', ran between Manchester and Bournemouth. The Great Western hated the S & D — the 'Slow and Dirty' as it was disparagingly known. Old railway rivalries die hard. When, finally, the Western Region of BR took over the running responsibility of the S & D from Southern Region, closure was inevitable. The descendants of the GWR had the final word, and the last hollow laugh, as a marvellous cross-country railway was debilitated, starved and killed. Yet the memory of the S & D will never, never die.

Our railways were sturdily built, and lines long since closed cannot be obliterated either from memory, or physically. Of the S & D much still remains for the discerning searcher. To seek and find old lines is melancholy, but rewarding. Wherever you are, you will doubtless find a local bookshop with a history book about the line that you have chosen to explore. In one fell swoop you can be an explorer, an historian, enjoy fresh air in the countryside and get to know in detail a piece of your own country which you may never have previously visited. There is no better territory than the 'Slow and Dirty', but those final months on the S & D were dismal days, as my chapter on Highbridge sets out to show.

From the Somerset & Dorset Joint Railway, let us travel almost as far away as it is possible to travel in Britain, to a place where stands the remains of one of Britain's strangest 'railway follies', the erstwhile Fort Augustus line. Opened on 22 July 1903, the line ran from Spean Bridge north-westwards through the Great Glen and then alongside Loch Lochy to Invergarry and Fort Augustus. Here, the company that

built the line, known as the Invergarry & Fort Augustus Railway, built its own pier and Pier station by Loch Ness, notwithstanding that berths for steamers plying on the Loch already existed. The railway ran — and the trackbed still runs — through thinly-populated countryside, yet it was built to main-line standards, with land purchased sufficient to build double track. There were two sturdy and expensive viaducts and numerous smaller bridges, as well as cuttings and tunnels. Undoubtedly the greatest folly, in every sense of the word, was the bridge over the River Oich, parallel to and nearby the Caledonian Canal, in Fort Augustus. At the time of construction it was only intended to run one train daily over this bridge to link the Town (village?) and Pier stations.

The promoters of the line planned — maybe dreamed is a better word — of extending the line further north-westwards to reach Inverness. Long before any such plans matured, the Highland Railway built its cut-off line from Aviemore to Inverness and thus destroyed any possible commercial *raison d'être* for the projected Fort Augustus-Inverness extension. Traffic to Fort Augustus itself never remotely reached the hoped-for levels of the promoters. On 30 September 1907, the Invergarry & Fort Augustus Railway management closed the pier and station at Fort Augustus.

The fate of the rest of the line was inexorably determined by these events. Wrangles, writs, passion and pleas notwithstanding, the line

Visible remains of the Somerset & Dorset Joint Railway will last for generations, but not these level-crossing gates, photographed in June 1980 at Edington Burtle. Note the Bridgwater Anglers sign. Edington and Burtle, two small and — until the S & D arrived — insignificant hamlets, gained 'prominence' when the branch thence to Bridgwater was built, making a junction with the original Somerset Central line to Highbridge. Now it slumbers again, but its place in railway history is assured, although the branch was, in truth, more a twig, and closed quietly in 1954.

Such is the nostalgic affection for the S & D that it engenders jealousy — what a memorial for a line about which more has probably been written, per mile, than any railway on earth.

The piers of the bridge over the River Oich at Fort Augustus will stand yet for generations; few more expensive, expansive and short-lived examples exist on our island rail network than the folly of the Fort Augustus line.

ceased operating amidst a plethora of newspaper headlines that were unique at the time, but commonplace fifty years later. 'Fort Augustus Isolated: the Railway to be Closed' proclaimed *The Dundee Advertiser* on 25 October 1910. In fact, the line was forced to recommence a service of sorts, illustrating the predicament of the railways under obligations laid down by Parliament. The line struggled on until 1 December 1933, when it was closed to all traffic save a weekly coal train which itself eventually gave up the ghost and the line was closed completely on 31 December 1946.

Fort Augustus had long beckoned me. It is a long way to travel in order to take photographs and inevitably one is at the mercy of the weather. My visit to the line took place in damp, misty conditions, and my arrival coincided with the onset of heavier rain, and thus miserable conditions for colour photography. Enquiries of the few locals around in such nasty weather quickly located the remains of the old bridge. Having 'yomped' across a rocky wasteland, I clambered up to the parapet and stared across the river at 'track' level. It was well worth the journey for anyone who hankers after the history of Britain's railway system at its remoter outposts.

In spite of protestations from my long-suffering wife Jane — twenty-seven years married to a railway enthusiast leaves most wives resigned to such far-flung excursions — we sought out and eventually discovered the site of the old Pier station, now restored to pristine condition as a dwelling, and at the time of our visit occupied by a most delightful young housewife. Evidence of the Loch Ness Pier is there aplenty. Incidentally, Fort Augustus is a delightful place with an Edwardian air. The multiple lock-gates on the Caledonian Canal are of interest, too.

Back to the railways, and back to the other end of Britain for my next memory of the railways of yesteryear. Known emotively as the 'Withered Arm', the London & South Western Railway poked a long, crooked finger into North Cornwall. The history of the LSWR's far-flung Cornish enterprise with the Bodmin & Wadebridge line opened in 1834. This long-detached part of the system was not joined up until 1895 by the LSWR's North Cornwall line. Passing through isolated places like Halwill Junction, in the middle of nowhere, and serving rural communities at stations like St Kew Highway and Port Isaac Road, the line eventually reached Wadebridge, where the erstwhile 'Atlantic Coast Express' made a final lunge to the ocean at Padstow, the Wadebridge-Padstow section of the line having opened on 27 March 1899. That final section of line, once the preserve of Drummond's splendid 'T9' express engines and latterly of Bulleid 'Pacifics', ran beside the Camel estuary and crossed Little Petherick Creek on a three-span iron bridge about half a mile short of the terminus at Padstow. That bridge has mercifully survived, and now forms part of a footpath where one's memory may, perhaps, recall those golden days when 'Padstow' still appeared on the train indicator-board at Waterloo. It seems a long time ago, albeit only just over twenty years, that 'Battle of Britain' or 'West Country' 'Pacifics' turned on Padstow's 70 ft turntable, itself installed as recently as 1947.

Britain abounds with historic old railway lines. Some are well known, others are secreted both by time and by the remoteness from centres of population or tourism. Not all are by any means available as public footpaths. Whither shall we wander next? If Fort Augustus and Padstow are geographically near the extremities of Britain, then Shropshire is quite the reverse, hidden deep in that strange borderland 'twixt North and South, West Midlands and Wales. To my shame I had never visited Salop until driven there in search of an odd old railway. The object of my visit was the south-east corner of the county, broadly described as the south Shropshire Hills. Here, Titterstone Clee and Brown Clee form the highest land in the county and their basalt-capped hills dominate an area of rolling, well-wooded agricultural countryside of isolated farms and sparsely-populated and scattered hamlets and villages.

In some ways, the Clee Hills remind one of Bodmin Moor, with their long history of mineral workings. It was to serve this industrial outcrop that the Cleobury Mortimer & Ditton Priors Light Railway (CMDP) was conceived, the history of which has long fascinated me and which finally dragged me to its tomb. The line was built at the beginning of the century and opened in 1908 — quite recently in railway terms — both to provide transport for the extensive quarrying operations and to serve the farming community. Absorbed by the Great Western Railway in 1922, the line retained its distinctive character. Its primary aim of exploiting the mineral deposits of the Clee Hills was nullified by the decline of stone traffic in the early 'thirties. Regular passenger services, never extensive or well-patronized, struggled to survive, failed, and succumbed in 1938. Indeed, only the war saved the line from extinction by the establishment of a Royal Naval Ammunition Depot (RNAD) at Ditton Priors. Following Beeching, the continued existence under BR of lines like the CMDP was unthinkable, even with RNAD Ditton Priors as the *raison d'être*. With the closure of the line from Tenbury Wells to Bewdley in 1964, the fate of the CMDP was sealed and the line closed, with little excitement and less fuss, at Easter 1965. An odd postscript to this little-known byway is that the track in and around Ditton Priors depot remained *in situ* after the closure of the branch up from Cleobury Mortimer, and the diesel shunters still pottered about a system isolated physically from the national BR network.

Twenty years later, a casual visitor would not know that the railway existed. Indeed, some of the owners of the former trackbed seem to delight in frustrating the tiny handful of those sufficiently interested in our country's history to make a pilgrimage there. Notwithstanding disinterested natives, hostile notices, overgrown trackbed and stretches of the line ploughed back into the fields whence they came, I recommend a visit. Before you go, buy a copy of *The Cleobury Mortimer and Ditton Priors Light Railway* by M.R.C. Price, published by the Oakwood Press; like most of the booklets in their list, it provides an exemplary insight into a selected corner of the railway map of Britain, albeit sadly, in the case of the CMDP, a corner almost forgotten.

Four years ago, I visited the dead city of Palmyra in the Syrian desert. Here, well preserved, stand the remains of one of the most magnificent of civilization's manifestations. From the ruins of the first-century Roman city to the Valley of the Tombs and its hilltop fortress, Palmyra is as beautiful as its more frequently visited Middle Eastern near contemporaries of Baalbek and Byblos, or even Jerash, and certainly more evocative. As, quite alone, I greeted the dawn, huddled incongruously into my dark blue overcoat against the desert cold, my mind wandered illogically to another, distant remnant of a bygone age — the scrapyard at Barry in South Wales where remained the last great hoard of metal leviathans of a vanished era.

My knowledge of architecture is limited to my personal taste. My interest in archaeology likewise has more to do with atmosphere and surroundings than with the subject itself. Yet my interest in industrial archaeology in general, and railway history in particular, is intense.

The call of those dismembered hulks, standing gaunt, pathetic and derelict in their South Wales graveyard, is strong, and I am not alone. Since the end of steam on British Rail in 1968, the scrapyard's owner, Dai Woodham, now rightly rewarded with an MBE, estimates that more than two million people, all unpaying, mostly uninvited, mostly trespassers, have visited his 'Gallic Palmyra'. Thus is measured the compelling call of steam, for in the year of my Syrian visit a mere 22,000 visited Palmyra albeit somewhat less accessible.

Steam in the landscape can be seen again, from north-east Scotland to south-west England, on preserved railways. Yet I cannot but admit that, for me, the glitter and sparkle of immaculate locomotives chuntering up and down a few miles of track unconnected to British Rail's main system fails to evoke the deep chord of emotion that attached me to the real railway in the steam era. In those days — and they were but two decades ago — the engines were often filthy, the steam locomotive depots crumbling, cracked and cruel in their contempt of a once great heritage of magnificence. That is probably why the lingering hulks inhabiting Dai Woodham's Barry graveyard evoke, for me, a deeper affection than the preserved railways. Perhaps it is the difference between Palmyra and Disneyland.

Quietly returning to nature: the Cleobury Mortimer & Ditton Priors Light Railway in August 1983 near Detton on this little-known backwater of rural England. Closure of obscure, little-used lines like this is understandable but the policy of selling off the trackbed has always infuriated me. The new owners of much of the CMDP, like innumerable others, are positively hostile to those who seek to explore the heritage of long-gone rural transport byways. Compared to the French, we are uncivilized, unimaginative and uncaring in this respect.

As steam's nadir approached, the regions of British Rail vied with each other for the dubious title of being the first to herald steam's extinction from their territory. Class after class of famous locomotives — 'Castles' and 'Kings' from the GWR, 'Jubilees' and 'Royal Scots' form the LMS, streamlined 'A4s' from the LNER and 'Merchant Navys' form the SR — were withdrawn. Scrapyards across Britain snapped up these leviathans from whom life had been extinguished when in truth they had years of useful service left. The mania for change saw smelly, unreliable diesels replace the reliable coal-burning steam engines.

To railway enthusiasts, the names of these scrapyards are burned into our souls: King's of Norwich, Cohen's of Kettering, Cashmore's of Great Bridge, Ward's of Sheffield, Draper's of Hull, McWilliam's of Shettleston. And of course many engines were cut up on site at the great railway workshops where some of them had been built: Cowlairs, Doncaster, Swindon, Darlington, Eastleigh. The melancholy task of destroying the world's greatest fleet of steam locomotives proceeded apace. Like dead bodies awaiting removal to the crematorium, engines, their fires dropped for the last time, waited in sombre rows at sheds whence they ran their last journeys, for the call to the last post. Yet at Barry was played out the most extraordinary final scene of this wanton act of railway vandalism.

During the 1960s, Dai Woodham purchased nearly 300 of British Rail's redundant steam fleet. At the same time, with steam's demise now an approaching cataclysm for innumerable enthusiasts, the era of railway preservation was emerging. In Yorkshire, the Keighley & Worth Valley Railway sought to emulate the efforts of the Bluebell Railway in Sussex. Within one month of steam's demise on BR, the first withdrawn locomotive left Barry. Former Midland Railway 0-6-0 No 43924, built in October 1920 and withdrawn by BR in July 1965, had arrived in South Wales in October of that year. Its fate seemed inevitable. Less than three years after arrival, however, came new life snatched from the jaws of death. The amazing saga of Woodhams had begun.

As the cutter's torch was inexorably wielded at other scrapyards, Woodhams turned their attention to cutting up redundant trucks, wagons and coaches. Time and the development of the preserved railways coincided and ultimately conspired to retain at Barry the only remaining collection of unrestored British steam locomotives.

I make no apology for my fervent attachment to Barry. Has there ever previously in history been a scrapyard that has become both a destination for pilgrims and a source for numerous books, magazine articles and television films? I doubt it. Dai Woodham himself, in his foreword to Alan Warren's admirable book *Rescued from Barry*, recalls how he and I, amongst others, founded the 'Barry 21 Club', with the stated objective of trying to rescue as many as possible of Barry's inmates from destruction. Our success has surprised no-one more than ourselves.

Barry has become extinct; we have found new homes for all the engines.

Both directly and by implication I have been criticized by others more active and worthy in railway preservation for concentrating time and energy on Barry's hulks rather than in specifically supporting the collective activities of the preserved railways. If this is a crime, then my guilt may be proven; but surely railway preservation, industrial archaeology itself, are matters of individual choice. Who am I, or who is anyone, to say that an individual should do this, that or the other with his recreational time?

Whilst many of the preserved railways can claim individual features to distinguish them from other lines, only Steamtown at Carnforth, six miles north of Lancaster, can genuinely claim to be unique. Home to the most famous steam locomotive in the world, LNER No 4472 *Flying Scotsman*, Carnforth was one of the last three steam engine sheds to remain in service until steam's final fling on British Rail in August 1968 (see '10A, 10D, 10F'). Covering some 23 acres, the site includes the working coaling-plant, a concrete structure once the hallmark of many engine sheds throughout Britain. In a key position adjacent to the main London-Glasgow line and the routes westwards to Barrow and eastwards to Skipton, Leeds and York, Carnforth acts as the source of motive power for many of the BR-organized steam excursions seen on the main lines, to which of course it is firmly attached.

Thanks to the dedication and determination of many people in all walks of life, there remains in Britain today plenty of steam in the landscape. But as time slips by, will the knowledge needed to maintain and indeed to propel the remaining steam locomotives wither? Or will it be handed down to a new generation of men and women whose experience of a 'real' steam railway is limited to anecdote? The evidence is that there is a shortage neither of teachers nor of pupils with the will to safeguard the future of steam. The threat lies in the actual condition of the locomotives themselves, as well as in the attitude of senior BR management to steam operations on their lines.

There is a magic about steam; an indefinable, inexplicable atmosphere of action, excitement, raw power. It will never die. Nor will the memory of those tracks, carved across Britain by men who were giants.

INDEX